Personal Statement - Still Becoming

[Collection of short literary works]

Written by Taria Fitch

Table of Contents

BECOMING: A Black Woman's Journey Through Identity, Survival, and Self-Discovery

INTRODUCTION: The Architecture of Self

Dear Reader,

What you're about to read isn't a memoir in the traditional sense. It's not a neat, linear story with a clear beginning, middle, and end. Life doesn't work that way—especially not for Black Women navigating a world that simultaneously fetishizes and fears us, that demands our strength while denying our humanity, that appropriates our culture while devaluing our lives.

This is a collection of truths. Some raw. Some refined. All real.

This is the story of becoming—not in the past tense, but in the present continuous. Because I'm not done. None of us are. We're all constantly in the process of becoming who we're meant to be, shedding who we thought we had to be, reclaiming who we were before the world told us who to be.

Who This Is For

This collection is for Black Women who are tired of being strong all the time.

It's for anyone who's ever felt like they had to split themselves into different versions to survive different spaces.

It's for survivors who are still figuring out what healing looks like.

It's for the girls who grew up too fast and the women still searching for the childhood that was stolen.

It's for anyone who's been called "too much" or "not enough" and is learning that both labels are lies.

It's for the people who contain multitudes and refuse to apologize for their complexity.

It's for the ones still writing letters to their future selves, hoping the journey gets easier (spoiler: it doesn't get easier, but you get stronger).

It's for anyone who's looked in the mirror and seen a stranger, then done the work to meet themselves again.

What You'll Find Here

This collection is organized not chronologically, but thematically—the way memory actually works, the way healing actually happens. Because trauma isn't linear. Growth isn't linear. Becoming isn't linear.

You'll find letters to my future self that chart the evolution from uncertainty to self-assurance, from performing to being present, from surviving to thriving. These letters capture the hope, the doubt, the determination of a Black woman carving out space for herself in 2024 and 2025.

You'll find declarations of identity that refuse to be contained in one box, one label, one expectation. "Little Miss Patricia" and the extended manifesto that demands you do your own deep excavation of self. Because you can't control your narrative if you don't know your story.

You'll find reflections on personal branding that challenge the notion that we have to choose between authenticity and strategy. "He Says, She Says" explores what it means to be seen, to be known, to ensure that who we are aligned with who we show up as in the world.

You'll find survival testimony that doesn't shy away from the ugliest truths. "From Silence to Fire to Self-Worth" is a reclamation—of voice, of body, of innocence, of power. It's for every survivor who's been told they're lying, attention-seeking, too sensitive, not credible. You are. You're all of those things the gaslighters say you're not.

You'll find the multiplicity of self celebrated rather than pathologized. "Mixed Personalities" introduces you to Alexis, Yvette, Loretta, and London— the various personas that emerge depending on context, need, and environment. Because containing multitudes isn't a disorder; it's a superpower.

You'll find sanctuaries mapped in "Threads"—the places and spaces where freedom lives. Country Aire teaches us about roots. Home on the Hill teaches us about chosen family. Bug teaches us about mobile sanctuary. Together, they teach us that home isn't one place—it's the thread connecting them all.

What Ties It All Together

Every piece in this collection, regardless of topic or tone, circles back to the same central questions:

Who am I when the world isn't watching?

Who am I when I strip away the performance, the code-switching, the survival mechanisms?

Who am I in my fullest, truest, most unapologetic form?

And how do I become that person consistently, courageously, without compromise?

These questions don't have simple answers. They require deep work—the kind of work I've been doing and documenting throughout these pieces. The kind of work I'm inviting you to do alongside me.

Why Now? Why This?

We're living in a moment where Black Women are simultaneously more visible and more vulnerable than ever. We're leading movements, breaking barriers, shattering glass ceilings. We're also dying at disproportionate rates during childbirth, facing the highest rates of violence, carrying the weight of everyone's expectations while our own needs go unmet.

We're expected to be strong—always. To be resilient—endlessly. To be gracious—even when we're being disrespected. To be forgiving—even when we haven't received apologies. To be everyone's backbone while our own spines are breaking.

In 2025, I'm saying: **enough.**

Enough performing strength when we need to be soft. Enough sacrificing our wellbeing for everyone else's comfort. Enough shrinking ourselves to fit into spaces that were never designed for us. Enough carrying shame that was never ours to begin with.

This collection is my refusal. My resistance. My reclamation.

And it's my invitation to you to do the same.

A Note on Vulnerability

Writing this collection required me to be vulnerable in ways that terrified me. To share the parts of my story that I usually keep private. To name the things I usually whisper. To claim the identities I usually hedge about.

There were moments I wanted to delete everything. Moments I worried about being "too much" or "too honest" or "too Black" or "too angry" or "too damaged" or "too complicated."

But then I remembered: **those "too much" labels are designed to silence us.**

So I chose to be too much. Too honest. Too Black. Too angry when anger is warranted. Too open about my damage and my healing. Too complicated to be easily categorized.

I chose to be whole, which means being all of myself—the light and the shadow, the healed and the healing, the powerful and the vulnerable, the certain and the still-figuring-it-out.

How to Read This Collection

There's no right way to engage with these pieces. You can read straight through or skip around. You can read one piece and sit with it for days before moving to the next. You can return to the ones that resonate and skip the ones that don't (yet—they might hit different later).

But I do have some suggestions:

Read with an open heart. Some of these pieces will be uncomfortable. They're meant to be. Discomfort is often where growth lives.

Read with a journal nearby. The reflection questions scattered throughout aren't rhetorical. They're invitations. Answer them. Do the work alongside me.

Read as a Black woman, or read as an ally. If you're a Black woman, I hope you see yourself in these pages and feel less alone. If you're not, I hope you gain insight into experiences different from your own and leave more committed to supporting Black Women's full humanity.

Read with compassion—for me and for yourself. We're all doing the best we can with what we have. Healing isn't pretty. Becoming isn't linear. Grace is required.

What I Hope You Take Away

If you walk away from this collection
with nothing else, I hope you walk away
with these truths:

You are not your trauma. What
happened to you is part of your story,
but it's not the whole story. You
survived. Now you get to decide who
you become.

You contain multitudes. Your
complexity is not a flaw. Your
multiplicity is not a disorder. You can be
many things—contradictory things—
and still be whole.

Your voice matters. Even when it shakes. Even when it's not perfectly articulated. Even when others try to silence it. Speak anyway.

Your anger is valid. Don't let anyone tell you to calm down, to be more palatable, to forgive before you're ready. Your anger is information. Your anger is fuel. Your anger is righteous.

Your healing is yours. It doesn't have to look like anyone else's. It doesn't have to follow a timeline. It doesn't have to include forgiveness or reconciliation. Your healing can be messy and nonlinear and uniquely yours.

You are enough. Not when you achieve more. Not when you heal more. Not when you become more. Right now. As you are. You are enough.

An Invitation to Becoming

This collection documents my becoming. But it's also an invitation to yours.

Throughout these pieces, you'll find questions, challenges, assignments. I'm asking you to do more than passively read—I'm asking you to actively engage. To excavate your own identity. To examine your own narratives. To explore your own personas. To map your own sanctuaries.

Because here's what I know for sure: **liberation is collective.**

My freedom is tied to yours is tied to theirs. When one of us does the work of becoming, it makes it easier for the next person. When one of us speaks truth, it creates space for others to speak theirs. When one of us refuses to shrink, it gives others permission to expand.

So this isn't just my story. It's our story. The story of Black Women—and all marginalized people—doing the sacred work of becoming who we were always meant to be, despite systems designed to prevent exactly that.

Before You Begin

Take a breath.

What you're about to read will be heavy at times. It will ask you to confront uncomfortable truths—about yourself, about society, about the work still required. It will demand vulnerability. It will challenge you to dig deeper than you might want to.

But it will also offer hope. It will celebrate resilience. It will affirm your experiences. It will remind you that you're not alone. It will show you that survival is possible, that transformation is real, that becoming is a lifelong journey worth taking.

So breathe. Ground yourself. Prepare for the journey.

Welcome to Becoming.

Welcome to the messy, beautiful, painful, powerful work of meeting yourself fully—past, present, and future.

Welcome to the collection that asks: Who are you? And who are you becoming?

The answer is on the following pages.

But more importantly, the answer is being written in your life, every single day.

Let's discover it together.

With love, rage, hope, and unapologetic Black excellence,

Taria Patricia Fitch
October 2025

Little Miss Patricia: A 2025 Manifesto of Self

The Question We All Need to Answer

Who am I? NO, the question should be who are YOU? I am not you nor are you me so again who am I? Well, I'll tell you who...

Wassup, my name is Taria, *or* Alexis, Loretta, Yvette, or Carmen depending on the day.

I AM the BEAUTIFUL BLACK AND EDUCATED woman standing before you today.

I AM from Markham, IL.

I AM a product of my community.

I AM that girl who had to be home before the streetlights came on.

I AM the baby of three who suffers from youngest sibling syndrome.

I AM my nicknames—POWERgirl, Reetabeeta, MyTarBaby, Gremlin, Lil Pat, TT, T and more.

I AM the sweet girl who was bullied because her tight coils shined so brightly and her clothes were "hand-me-downs".

I AM the pure kid who had to protect her innocence away from monsters.

I AM a sexual assault survivor.

I AM the girl who loves getting her scalp scratched by her grandma.

I AM the kid who loved to eat hot crunchy curls until they made my stomach footwork.

I AM the girl who would ask for all her cousins' for their pocket change to save for the candy store across the street.

I AM the girl around Country Aire who everyone knows and looks out for because of my family's reputation and the way I carry myself.

I AM just a girl.

I AM a proud member of the bisexual community.

I AM a hopeless romantic.

I AM very self-reflective.

I AM a reliable friend.

I AM still learning.

I AM the one all my family comes to vent to about whatever.

I AM extremely inquisitive.

I AM a young adult still understanding her worth.

I AM a leader.

I AM a very emotional person, some would say "crybaby" I say haters.

I AM dependable and nurturing.

I AM the one you want in your corner.

I AM a fruit-o-holic.

I AM an advocate for equity.

I AM making way for those who come after me.

I AM human.

I AM the kid who grew up and still loves to watch crime shows Leverage, White Collar, Blacklist, Hawaii 5-O, and Dexter (if you know you know).

I AM spoiled in love and affection.

I AM a friend who likes to give and receive random gifts of appreciation.

I AM the friend who makes big posters and yells at your sports games and root for all your achievements.

I AM a WOMAN who will not allow anyone to take advantage of me.

I AM a godmother and auntie.

I AM breaking generational curses and barriers.

I AM a young adult who dreams big no matter how far-fetched it may sound.

I AM T-A-R-I-A and you will address me correctly.

I AM a support system.

I AM a reflection of my beautiful mother in more ways than physical appearance.

I AM a young adult who stands up for herself by any means necessary.

I AM an inspiring Therapist.

I AM tropicaljuice._

I AM full of love.

I AM Taria Patricia Fitch, and the new question is why be someone else when I can be me?

Now It's Your Turn: Dig Deeper

Listen, if you made it this far, you already know what time it is. This isn't just my story—this is a call to action. This is me standing in my full, complicated, beautiful truth and demanding that you do the same.

The Work Begins With You

In 2026, we don't have time for the surface-level "I'm fine" conversations anymore. We're going deeper. We're asking the hard questions. We're sitting with the uncomfortable answers. We're excavating the parts of ourselves we've buried because someone told us they were too much, not enough, or too hard to love.

Who are you? Not who your parents wanted you to be. Not who your partner needs you to be. Not who your job requires you to be. Not who social media filters you into. Not who trauma molded you into. But who are YOU?

Strip it all away. The degrees. The job titles. The relationship status. The follower counts. The achievements. The masks. The code-switching. The performance. What's left? That's where the real work begins.

Questions You Need to Ask Yourself (And Answer Honestly)

What parts of myself have I hidden to make others comfortable?

Think about it. Really think. How many times have you made yourself smaller so someone else could feel bigger? How many times have you dimmed your light so you wouldn't be "too much"? How many times have you swallowed your truth because speaking it might rock the boat? In 2026 and beyond, we're done shrinking. We're done apologizing for taking up space. We're done muting our voices for people who were never going to listen anyway.

What stories about myself have I believed that were never mine to begin with?

We carry narratives that don't belong to us. Stories about what Black Women should be. Stories about strength meaning silence. Stories about worthiness being conditional. Stories about our bodies, our hair, our culture, our love, our pain. Who wrote these stories? Probably not us. So why are we still living by someone else's script? It's time to rewrite the narrative. Your story, your pen, your truth.

What am I afraid people will see if I show up authentically?

This is the big one. The scary one. Because authenticity is vulnerable. It means people might not like what they see. It means rejection is possible. It means you might lose people who only loved the version of you that served their needs. But here's the thing: those aren't your people anyway. Your real tribe? They're waiting for the real you to show up so they can finally recognize you.

What does healing actually look like for me, not what Instagram tells me it should look like?

Healing isn't always yoga and green smoothies and gratitude journals—though if that's your thing, do you. Healing might be messy. It might be therapy sessions where you ugly cry. It might be setting boundaries that piss people off. It might be cutting off family members who are toxic. It might be taking medication. It might be rage and grief and laughter all in the same day. Your healing journey doesn't need to be aesthetic or inspirational. It just needs to be yours.

What generational patterns am I repeating without even realizing it?

Look at your family. Look at the women who came before you. What did they teach you about love? About pain? About worthiness? About survival? Some of those lessons served them well in their time. Some of those lessons are killing you slowly in yours. It's okay to honor their struggle while choosing a different path. Breaking generational curses doesn't mean you love your ancestors any less. It means you love yourself and your future enough to do the work they couldn't.

What would I do if I wasn't afraid?

Fear is a liar. Fear tells you to play it safe. Fear tells you to stay small. Fear tells you that comfort is better than growth. Fear tells you that you're not ready, not worthy, not enough. But what if fear wasn't driving? What if courage took the wheel? What would you create? Where would you go? Who would you become? What dreams would you chase? Write it down. Make it real. Then do one small thing today that scares you.

Where am I performing versus where am I present?

We perform all day, every day. At work. On social media. In relationships. Sometimes even for ourselves. Performance is exhausting. Presence is powerful. Presence means being fully in your body, in your truth, in your moment, without apology or explanation. When was the last time you were truly present? Not documenting for the 'gram. Not worrying about how you look or sound. Not calculating your next move. Just being. Find those moments. Multiply them.

The Mirror Test

Here's an exercise for you. Stand in front of a mirror. Look yourself in the eyes. Really look. Not at your hair or your outfit or that thing you wish you could change about your body. Look into your eyes. The windows to your soul, right?

Now say: "I AM _____."

Fill in the blank. Not with what you do, but with who you are. Not with your roles, but with your essence. Not with your trauma, but with your triumph. Not with your past, but with your present. Not with your performance, but with your truth.

Say it until you believe it. Say it until it feels less like a declaration and more like a remembering. Because that's what this work is—remembering who you were before the world told you who to be.

The "I AM" Revolution

You saw my list. Now make yours. Not the pretty, polished, LinkedIn-ready version. The real, raw, messy, complicated, beautiful, broken, healing, whole version. Include the contradictions. You can be both soft and fierce. You can be both healing and hurting. You can be both confident and uncertain. You can be both the trauma and the triumph.

Your "I AM" statements are your armor and your weapon. They're how you ground yourself when the world tries to shake you. They're how you remember your power when systems try to strip it away. They're how you claim your space when society tries to erase you.

For My Black Women Reading This

This is especially for us. Because we carry extra weight. We navigate extra obstacles. We fight extra battles. And we're expected to do it all with grace and a smile and without ever showing that we're tired.

Who are you underneath the "strong Black woman" stereotype? Who are you when you're not being everyone's backbone? Who are you when you're not code-switching or translating or performing respectability? Who are you in the quiet moments when no one's watching and no one's judging and you can finally exhale?

You are not what happened to you. You are not the trauma. You are not the struggle. You are not the systems that tried to break you. You survived all of that, yes, but you are so much more than your survival.

You are magic. You are power. You are worthy—not because of what you do or how you serve others, but because you exist. Your existence is resistance. Your joy is rebellion. Your rest is revolutionary. Your truth is transformative.

The Challenge

I dare you to get uncomfortable. I dare you to dig deeper than you ever have. I dare you to ask yourself the questions you've been avoiding. I dare you to sit with the answers even when they hurt. I dare you to stop performing and start being present. I dare you to choose yourself, unapologetically and consistently.

Write your own manifesto. Say your own truth. Claim your own identity. Not for social media. Not for applause. But for you. For your healing. For your freedom. For your future.

Because here's what I know for sure: when you know who you are—I mean really know, deep in your bones, unshakeable truth—nobody can tell you who to be. When you own your story, nobody can weaponize it against you. When you claim your identity, nobody can steal your power.

The Connection

This work—this deep, soul-level excavation of self—it's the foundation for everything else. You can't build authentic community if you're not being authentic. You can't demand respect if you don't respect yourself. You can't break cycles if you don't understand the cycles you're in. You can't be present for others if you're not present with yourself.

Everything connects. Your past informs your present which shapes your future. Your individual healing contributes to collective liberation. Your personal truth becomes part of our shared story. Your courage to be yourself gives someone else permission to do the same.

We're all connected in this struggle, in this journey, in this work of becoming. Your liberation is tied to mine is tied to hers is tied to theirs. When one of us rises, we all rise. When one of us heals, we all heal. When one of us breaks free, we all get a little bit closer to freedom.

The Final Word

So again, I ask you: who are you?

Not who you were. Not who you wish you were. Not who you're trying to be. But who you are, right now, in this moment, in all your complicated glory?

When you figure it out—and you will, because you're doing the work—own it. Speak it. Live it. Be it. Unapologetically. Boldly. Authentically.

Because the world doesn't need another version of someone else. The world needs YOU. The real you. The whole you. The healed and healing you. The messy and magical you. The human you.

I AM Taria Patricia Fitch, standing in my truth, owning my story, claiming my power.

Now tell me: **WHO ARE YOU?**

And why would you ever want to be anyone else?

This manifesto is dedicated to every person searching for themselves in a world that profits from their confusion. May you find your truth. May you speak your truth. May you live your truth. May you BE your truth.

The revolution starts within.

He Says, She Says: Controlling Your Narrative in 2025

Hey Alexa, play Q.U.E.E.N. by Janelle Monae featuring Erykah Badu.

The Voices Around Us

They say what they say based on what they know (or think they know).

They say what they say because of what they have observed.

They say what they say because of what they have been told.

They say what they say because of what has been learned about me.

I can conjure a guess of what they may say, but that contradicts the principle "don't put words in other people's mouths." Taking that accepted and respected principle from my upbringing, I will not put words in others' mouths or minds. Instead, let's ask them what THEY say about me.

Below is a list of responses to the question, "What would you say about Taria?"

What They See

From a college friend: "Taria is a *distinctive* individual, known for her **unique approach to life**. Her capacity to extend her thoughts beyond herself is truly inspiring and commendable, showcasing her ability to transcend self-interest. She possesses a blend of intellect and abstract thinking as she approaches each day with *intention!* Taria's dedication to her endeavors sets a high standard for her aspirations. Take, for example, her initiative in bringing NACWC Light to Denison's campus, creating a vibrant space for black excellence to flourish. Taria epitomizes a visionary, radiating positivity wherever she goes and uplifting those in her midst. Despite the adversity she has faced, she remains resolutely optimistic."

From a schoolmate: "Taria is one of a kind—you meet people left and right and only a select few stick with you where you want to constantly keep in touch. No matter the circumstance she is always there to support you or lift you. If you're having a bad day, no matter how busy or stressed Taria is, she will make sure you are heard and will instantly make you feel like it's the sunniest day out. From little jokes to deep hour-long conversations you will never not enjoy time with her. I met her a year ago but it feels like I have known her for years and our friendship does not feel forced as a result of a common institution or job but rather a true and genuine **friendship** where there is trust, respect, kindness, and love all over."

From my favorite cousin (we'll call her Nuk): "Tari is... so many things. Her personality is **radiant**, & she's always 100% her authentic self. She's fun & funny— one thing she's going to do is laugh. Taria is a sweetheart. She's warm, and thoughtful, & brings me a sense of joy & peace whenever we're together. She's wise & mature for her age, an intellectual & a conversationalist for sure. I've watched Taria grow into a beautiful young woman who's creative, confident & driven. Although I'm older by 6 years, Taria has a way of allowing me to be vulnerable & I value her ideas & opinions. There isn't enough I can say about Taria, but she's my sister-like cousin who's also the homegirl."

From a younger friend: "Meeting you a few years ago and being so young I can truly say you taught me to live in my own truth. At such a young age you were unapologetically you and it was a breath of fresh air."

From a friend and mentee: "Taria brings good vibes wherever she goes. She is very real about life and always herself/natural. I think she is someone easy to be around because her comfort with herself makes it easy to be comfortable with her too. Taria is really honest and blunt but only ever has the best intentions with what she says. She just gives off 'cool big sister' energy and is a good person to have in your corner always."

The Mirror and The Window

Reading these responses hit different. Because here's the thing—I know who I am. I declared it in "Little Miss Patricia." I own my identity, my story, my truth. But there's something powerful about seeing yourself through the eyes of the people who witness you daily. It's like holding up a mirror and a window at the same time.

The mirror reflects what I know about myself. The window reveals what I'm projecting into the world.

And you know what? They match.

That's not an accident. That's intentional. That's what happens when you do the deep work of knowing yourself and then have the courage to show up as that person consistently. That's personal branding at its finest—not the manufactured, curated, fake-it-till-you-make-it kind. The authentic, this-is-who-I-am-take-it-or-leave-it kind.

The Truth About Personal Branding

Let's have a real conversation about this "personal brand" thing that everyone's always talking about. In 2025, we're bombarded with messages about crafting our image, curating our feeds, optimizing our LinkedIn profiles, building our platforms. And sure, some of that matters. But here's what matters more:

Your personal brand is not what you say about yourself. It's what others say about you when you're not in the room.

Read that again. Let it sink in.

You can post all the inspirational quotes you want. You can write the perfect bio. You can have the aesthetic feed. You can say you're a leader, a visionary, a change-maker. But if the people who actually know you—who see you when the cameras are off, when the pressure's on, when life gets messy—if they're not saying the same things? Your brand is a lie.

And in 2025, people can smell inauthenticity from a mile away.

What I Learned From Asking

When I decided to ask the people in my life what they'd say about me to a stranger, I was nervous. Not because I didn't think they'd have nice things to say, but because I was opening myself up to see the gap between who I think I am and who they experience me as.

What if they saw something different? What if my intentions didn't match my impact? What if I was performing a version of myself that I thought was authentic but was really just another mask?

But here's what happened: **consistency**.

The words that kept showing up—authentic, radiant, real, intentional, genuine, unapologetically herself. Those are the words I'd use to describe who I'm trying to be. The fact that they're the words others use to describe who I am? That's the work paying off.

But let me break down what each of these responses taught me:

Lesson 1: Your Impact Ripples Beyond Your Intention

My college friend talked about me extending my thoughts beyond myself, creating spaces for Black excellence, being a visionary. That's not just about me—that's about what I create for others. Your personal brand isn't selfish. When you show up fully, when you do the work, when you lead with intention, you create space for others to do the same. Your authenticity gives others permission to be authentic.

Your courage inspires others to be courageous. Your excellence elevates everyone around you.

Lesson 2: Consistency Builds Trust

My schoolmate mentioned that our friendship doesn't feel forced, that I'm always there no matter the circumstance. Here's the thing about personal branding—it's not about being perfect. It's about being consistent. People trust you when they know what they're getting. When you show up the same way on your best days and your worst days. When your private self matches your public self. When you're not one person on social media and a different person in real life.

Lesson 3: Authenticity Is Magnetic

Nuk (my favorite cousin, and if you know, you know) said I'm "always 100% her authentic self" and that I allow him to be vulnerable despite being younger. This is the power of authenticity—it disarms people. It makes space for real connection. When you're not performing, others don't have to perform either. When you're comfortable with yourself, you make others comfortable. When you're vulnerable, you give others permission to be vulnerable too. Authenticity isn't just about you—it's about creating an environment where everyone can be real.

Lesson 4: You're Always Teaching

My younger friend said I taught her to live in her truth just by being unapologetically myself. I wasn't trying to teach. I was just being. But that's the thing—you're always teaching. Especially as Black Women, especially as young people navigating spaces that weren't built for us, especially as people who choose authenticity in a world that profits from our insecurity. Someone is always watching. Someone is always learning. Someone is always taking notes on how you move through the world.

Lesson 5: Realness Is Your Superpower

My mentee talked about me being "very real about life" and giving off "cool big sister energy." In a world full of filters, facades, and fake it till you make it, being real is revolutionary. Being honest is powerful. Being blunt (with good intentions) is refreshing. People are starving for realness. They're exhausted from the performance.

When you show up real, you become a safe space. You become the person people want in their corner.

The Contradiction: Control vs. Authenticity

Here's where it gets interesting. I'm telling you that you control your personal brand, that you determine what others see and say about you. But I'm also telling you to be authentic, to be real, to stop performing.

Isn't that a contradiction?

No. And here's why:

Controlling your narrative doesn't mean controlling who you are. It means being so clear about who you are that your actions consistently reflect it.

Think about it. If I'm unclear about my values, I'll make decisions that contradict each other. If I don't know what I stand for, I'll stand for anything (or nothing at all). If I'm not intentional about who I want to be, I'll become whoever the situation demands.

But when I do the work—the deep, uncomfortable work of figuring out who I am, what matters to me, what I value, what I stand for—then controlling my narrative becomes simple. Not easy, but simple. Because every decision, every action, every interaction flows from that core understanding of self.

I don't have to remember what lie I told or what mask I wore in what situation. I just have to be me. Consistently. Intentionally. Unapologetically.

The Real Question: What Do People Say About You?

Now it's your turn. And this is where it gets uncomfortable.

If I asked the people in your life—your family, your friends, your coworkers, your schoolmates, your neighbors—"What would you say about [your name]?" what would they say?

More importantly: **Would their answers align with how you see yourself?**

Let me give you some scenarios to consider:

Scenario 1: The Performer You think you're authentic, but others describe you as "hard to read" or "always has it together" or "seems perfect." That gap? That's the performance showing. You're so busy curating the image that you've lost the substance. People sense it even if they can't name it.

Scenario 2: The Confused You're not sure who you are yet, and it shows. People describe you in contradictory ways because you show up differently in different spaces. You code-switch not just in how you speak, but in your entire personality. One person thinks you're outgoing, another thinks you're shy. One says you're confident, another says you're insecure. That inconsistency? It's a sign you haven't done the identity work yet.

Scenario 3: The Intentional You know who you are, and others' descriptions align with your self-understanding. There's consistency across contexts. The words they use to describe you match your values.

The impact they describe matches your intentions.
That alignment? That's mastery.

Building Your Brand: The Blueprint

If you want to control your narrative—if you want what people say about you to reflect who you actually are—here's the work:

Step 1: Know Yourself (For Real)

Not who you wish you were. Not who you're trying to be. Not who your parents want you to be or who social media says you should be. Who you actually are. Go back to "Little Miss Patricia." Do that work. Write your "I AM" statements. Dig deep. Get uncomfortable. Be honest.

Step 2: Define Your Values

What matters to you? What will you compromise on and what won't you? What do you stand for? What do you stand against? Your values are your compass. When you're clear on them, decision-making becomes easier. You don't have to wonder what to do—you just ask, "Does this align with my values?"

Step 3: Show Up Consistently

This is where most people fumble. They know who they are (or think they do), but they don't show up as that person consistently. They're authentic at home but perform at work. They're real with friends but fake on social media. They're vulnerable in therapy but guarded everywhere else.

Consistency builds trust. Consistency creates your reputation. Consistency is what makes your brand recognizable.

Step 4: Be Intentional About Your Impact

Every interaction is an opportunity to reinforce your brand. Every conversation, every post, every email, every meeting. I'm not saying be performative—I'm saying be intentional. Ask yourself: "Is this aligned with who I say I am? Is this the impact I want to have? Is this the person I want to be?"

Step 5: Check Your Mirrors

Periodically, check in. Ask people you trust what they'd say about you. Not for validation—for calibration. To make sure there's alignment between who you think you are and who you're showing up as. To catch your blind spots. To see if your intentions match your impact.

Step 6: Adjust as You Grow

Your brand isn't static. You're not static. As you grow, as you learn, as you evolve, your brand will too. That's okay. That's expected. That's healthy. The key is being intentional about the evolution. Deciding who you want to become and then doing the work to become that person.

The Danger Zone: When Brands Don't Match Reality

Let's talk about what happens when there's a disconnect between your brand and your reality. Because in 2025, that gap will get exposed. Quickly.

The "Woke" Performative: You post all the right things on social media, use all the right hashtags, say all the right words. But in real life? You don't show up. You don't do the work. You don't check your friends when they're out of line. You don't support the causes you claim to care about. People see through it. And when they do, your credibility is shot.

The "Strong Independent Woman" Who's Actually Struggling: You've built a brand around having it all together, being unbothered, being strong. But you're drowning. You're burnt out. You're barely holding it together. That facade will crack, and when it does, it'll hurt worse because you've isolated yourself. You've made it impossible for people to support you because you've convinced them you don't need support.

The "Nice Girl" Who's Actually Bitter: You smile, you're polite, you never rock the boat. But underneath? You're resentful. You're angry. You're keeping score. Eventually, that poison leaks out. In passive-aggressive comments. In sudden explosions. In relationships that deteriorate because people realize the "nice" was just a mask.

The "Mysterious" One Who's Just Closed Off: You think you're intriguing, complex, hard to read. But really? You're just emotionally unavailable. You've mistaken walls for boundaries. You've confused secrecy with privacy. People don't find you interesting—they find you exhausting.

The danger in all these scenarios is the same: **When who you say you are doesn't match who you actually are, eventually the truth comes out. And the fallout is worse than if you'd just been real from the start.**

The Black Woman's Burden: Branding Under Scrutiny

Now let me address the elephant in the room. Because everything I'm saying about personal branding? It hits different for Black Women.

We're always under scrutiny. Our appearance, our tone, our hair, our bodies, our ambition, our emotions—everything is analyzed, criticized, and weaponized. We're too much or not enough. Too loud or too quiet. Too aggressive or too passive. Too professional or too casual. We can't win.

So we perform. We code-switch. We mold ourselves to fit into spaces that were never designed for us. We learn to be palatable, non-threatening, digestible. We master the art of being "professional" which really just means "not too Black."

And in that process, we lose ourselves.

So when I talk about controlling your narrative, about building your brand, about being authentic—I know it's complicated for us. Because authenticity as a Black woman in predominantly white spaces can cost you opportunities, relationships, safety.

But here's what I learned: **The cost of performing is higher.**

When you perform, you're always exhausted. Always on guard. Always calculating. Always wondering if they see through it. Always knowing that if they do, if you slip up, if the mask falls, you'll be labeled "difficult" or "angry" or "unprofessional."

When you're authentic, you're free. You might face consequences—real ones. You might lose opportunities. But you'll keep your soul. You'll attract people and opportunities that want the real you. You'll build relationships based on truth, not transaction. You'll be able to rest because you're not maintaining a facade.

And here's the thing: **Your authenticity becomes your competitive advantage.**

In a sea of Black Women trying to assimilate, trying to code-switch their way to acceptance, trying to perform respectability—when you show up authentic, you stand out. Not because you're trying to stand out, but because you're not trying to blend in.

Look at the words people used to describe me: distinctive, unique, authentic, real, radiant, genuine, unapologetically herself. Those aren't words you earn by performing. Those are words you earn by being.

The Assignment: Your Brand Audit

Ready to do the work? Here's your assignment:

Part 1: Self-Assessment Write down 10 words you'd use to describe yourself. Not aspirational words— actual words. Who are you right now?

Part 2: The Ask Ask at least 5 people in your life (family, friends, coworkers, mentors) this question: "If a stranger asked you about me, what would you say?" Tell them to be honest. Prepare yourself to hear things that might not match your self-perception.

Part 3: The Gap Analysis Compare your list to theirs. Where's the alignment? Where's the gap? The alignment is your strength—double down on it. The gap is your work—investigate it.

Part 4: The Investigation For every gap, ask yourself:

- Is this who I actually am but I'm not showing it?
- Is this who I think I am but I'm not actually being?

- Is this who I want to be but I haven't become yet?
- Is this a perception I need to correct?
- Is this a reality I need to change?

Part 5: The Action Plan Based on your gap analysis, create an action plan. What needs to change? What needs to be amplified? What needs to be released? What needs to be developed?

Part 6: The Commitment Make a commitment to yourself. To be more intentional. To be more consistent. To be more authentic. Write it down. Date it. Hold yourself accountable.

The Truth About Opinions

Here's what I want you to remember: **People will always have opinions about you. Always.**

Some will love you. Some will hate you. Some will misunderstand you. Some will try to box you in. Some will project their insecurities onto you. Some will be threatened by you. Some will try to dim your light.

And you know what? **That's not your problem.**

Your problem—no, not problem—your responsibility is to show up as yourself. Consistently. Authentically. Unapologetically.

You can't control what people think about you. But you can control who you are. And when who you are is solid, when your foundation is strong, when your values are clear, when your actions are consistent— other people's opinions lose their power.

They can say what they want. As long as you know your truth, as long as the people who matter know your truth, as long as your reputation matches your reality— you're good.

The Connection: From Self to Community

Everything connects. Remember?

The work you did in "Little Miss Patricia"—that deep excavation of self—that feeds into this. You can't control your narrative if you don't know your story. You can't show up authentically if you don't know who you authentically are. You can't be consistent if you're not clear.

And this work? It feeds into what comes next. Because when you're solid in yourself, when your brand is aligned with your truth, when you show up consistently—you become a leader. Not because you're trying to be, but because people naturally follow those who are grounded in their truth.

Your personal brand isn't about you. It's about what you create in the world. It's about the space you hold for others. It's about the permission you give people to be themselves. It's about the impact you have on the lives you touch.

When people describe me, they don't just talk about me—they talk about how I make them feel, what I create for them, the space I hold, the energy I bring. That's what matters. That's what a real brand is.

The Final Word

So, what do people say about you?

Better question: **What do you want people to say about you?**

Even better question: **Are you being the person that would earn those descriptions?**

Your personal brand is your legacy in real-time. It's the impression you leave. It's the way people feel when they think of you. It's what they say when you're not in the room.

You control that. Not by manipulating your image, but by being intentional about who you are and showing up as that person consistently.

Be so clear about who you are that others can't help but see it too.

Be so consistent in your authenticity that your reputation becomes unshakeable.

Be so grounded in your truth that other people's opinions become background noise.

I AM Taria Patricia Fitch, and the people in my life confirm what I already know about myself.

Now: **WHO ARE YOU?** And what are the people in your life saying about you?

The answer should match. If it doesn't, you have work to do.

Get to it.

"And hey, I'm just being myself (What you say?). I'm just being myself (Say it, oh). I'm just being myself (Hey, hey, hey, hey). Am I a freak for dancing 'round? Am I a freak for getting down?"

— Janelle Monáe, "Q.U.E.E.N."

The revolution is being yourself in a world that wants you to be someone else. Control your narrative by knowing who you are and showing up as that person. Always.

From Silence to Fire to Self-worth:

A Reclamation

Part 1: The Stranger in the Mirror

My reflection in the chipped mirror was a stranger.

Anger, a coiled viper, lived in my gut, twisting every thought. It started with his clammy hand, the whispered promises that turned into a chilling nightmare. When I told his mom, her eyes went cold, the words "attention-seeking" a slap in the face. The viper tightened its grip.

The school was a battlefield. Jokes about "weaklings" echoed in the hallways, each one a fresh wound. Art class, my only escape, became a canvas for the storm inside. Black swirls choked vibrant colors, mirroring the suffocating silence around my truth.

One day, Ms. Reyes, my art teacher, stopped me after the bell chimed. Her gaze wasn't judgmental, but... seeing? "The anger," she said gently, "it's raw, powerful. Use it."

That night, I didn't paint black. I painted fire.

Orange flames licked the canvas, a phoenix rising from the ashes. It wasn't pretty, but it was honest. Ms. Reyes hung it in the school gallery. Nervousness gnawed at me, but when I saw kids whispering, their eyes wide, a spark ignited within. The fire resonated.

The viper loosened its hold that day. Maybe my art wasn't healing Mom, but it was speaking for me, a voice she refused to hear. People saw the pain and anger, but also a strength I didn't know I possessed. It wasn't a complete victory, but a small spark in the darkness.

As I looked in the mirror again, the stranger was fading. A fighter, though bruised, was staring back. The viper might not be gone, but the fire was mine to control.

Part II: The Language of Flames

Days turned into weeks, and the whispers in the hallways transformed. Instead of taunts, there were questions. Teachers and classmates approached me, curious about the "whys" behind my art. I shared sparingly, guarded by the scars of betrayal. But the act of creating, of pouring my pain onto canvas, felt liberating.

But the silence at home remained a constant ache. His mom would not acknowledge the paintings, the unspoken accusation hanging heavy in the air. Dinner conversations were strangled silences punctuated by the clatter of silverware. Her eyes, once a warm well of love, now held an unknown distance.

The viper of doubt tightened its coils again. Did she see the truth in my art, the betrayal etched in every brushstroke? Or did she see nothing, her denial a thick, impenetrable wall?

The school gallery became a stage for my silent scream, and the fire in my art had transformed. It was still there, a flicker of defiance, but now it was tempered with a newfound hope. It wasn't a complete healing, not yet. But the viper of doubt loosened its grip further, replaced by a burgeoning sense of self-worth.

Part III: What Fire Teaches You

Fire doesn't apologize for burning.

Fire doesn't ask permission to exist.

Fire doesn't shrink itself to make others comfortable.

I learned this slowly, painfully, through every brushstroke that refused to stay within the lines. Through every color that refused to be muted. Through every canvas that refused to lie.

The anger was my teacher before it became my weapon. Before it became my torch.

People want you to be quiet about the things that hurt. They want you to swallow the pain, to smile through the trauma, to protect the people who didn't protect you. They want you to carry the shame that was never yours to begin with. They want you to be small, manageable, easy to dismiss.

But fire refuses to be dismissed.

I painted because I couldn't speak. The words caught in my throat, tangled up with fear and shame and the desperate need to be believed. But the paint flowed freely. The colors didn't judge. The canvas didn't call me a liar. The art didn't ask me to prove what happened or explain why I didn't fight harder or question why I didn't scream louder.

The art just... held it. All of it. The rage. The grief. The violation. The betrayal—both the initial one and the second one, the one that came from not being believed, from being labeled "attention-seeking," from watching someone choose their comfort over my truth.

That second betrayal? Sometimes it cuts deeper than the first.

Part IV: The Reclamation

Let me tell you what they don't tell you about surviving:

Survival is not passive.

Survival is waking up every day and choosing yourself even when the world has shown you that you're not worth choosing. Survival is looking at the shattered pieces of your innocence and deciding that you're going to create something beautiful from the wreckage. Survival is refusing to let what happened to you become the only thing about you.

I didn't just survive. I transformed.

The girl in the chipped mirror—the stranger with dead eyes and a coiled viper in her gut—she had every right to stay angry. She had every right to let the rage consume her. She had every right to become bitter, closed off, a cautionary tale about what happens when you trust the wrong person.

But that's not who I became.

I became the phoenix in my painting. I became the fire itself.

I reclaimed my anger. Not the toxic kind that destroys everything in its path, but the righteous kind that says "this was wrong, and I will not pretend it wasn't." The kind that fuels change instead of feeding destruction. The kind that lights the way for others stumbling through their own darkness.

I reclaimed my voice. Even when it shook. Even when it cracked. Even when speaking my truth cost me relationships I thought I couldn't live without. Because silence is not peace.

Silence is not protection. Silence is complicity in your own erasure.

I reclaimed my body. The one that was violated. The one that carried the trauma in every cell. The one that flinched at unexpected touch. I learned that it was still mine. That what happened to it didn't define it. That healing doesn't mean forgetting—it means integrating. It means carrying the scars while refusing to let them dictate your future.

I reclaimed my innocence. Not the naive kind that got taken from me—that's gone, and I've made peace with that loss. But the innocent belief that I deserved safety, respect, bodily autonomy. The innocent truth that what happened was not my fault. The innocent knowledge that my worth was never tied to someone else's violence.

I reclaimed my story. For too long, other people held the narrative. He held it with his lies. His mother held it with her denial. The school held it with their jokes and their silence. But my art gave me the pen back. My healing gave me authority over my own narrative. This is my story, and I get to tell it how I choose.

Part V: For Those Still in the Darkness

If you're reading this and you see yourself in these words—if you know what it's like to be called a liar, to be labeled "attention-seeking," to have your truth dismissed by the very people who should have protected you—I need you to hear this:

You are not crazy. The gaslighting, the denial, the minimizing—that's about their discomfort, not your truth. Trust yourself. Trust your body. Trust your memory. You know what happened.

You are not alone. Even when it feels like you're drowning in silence, even when no one else will say it out loud, you are not alone. There is a whole army of survivors who believe you, who see you, who know exactly what it feels like to have your trauma denied.

You are not damaged goods. You are not broken beyond repair. You are not less than. What happened to you was a violation, yes. It changed you, yes. But it did not destroy your worth. Your value is inherent. It cannot be taken by violence or erased by betrayal.

Your anger is valid. Let me say that louder for the people in the back: **YOUR ANGER IS VALID.** You don't have to forgive. You don't have to "rise above." You don't have to perform healing for anyone's comfort. Your anger is a rational response to an irrational situation. Let it fuel you. Let it protect you. Let it transform you.

Your healing is yours. It doesn't have to look like anyone else's. It doesn't have to follow a timeline. It doesn't have to include forgiveness or reconciliation or understanding. Your healing can be messy. It can be nonlinear. It can include therapy and medication and art and rage and tears and laughter and all the contradictions that make us human.

You will survive this. I can't promise it won't hurt. I can't promise it will be easy. I can't promise everyone will believe you or that justice will be served or that the people who failed you will suddenly wake up and apologize. But I can promise you this: you are stronger than you know. You contain multitudes. You

can hold both the pain and the joy, the trauma
and the triumph, the past and the future.

You are already a survivor. Every day you
wake up and keep going? That's an act of
resistance. Every time you choose yourself?
That's an act of rebellion. Every moment you
refuse to let what happened define you?
That's an act of revolution.

Part VI: What I Know Now

The chipped mirror is still there. Sometimes I
still see echoes of the stranger. The viper still
lives in my gut—I don't think it will ever fully
leave. Trauma doesn't work like that. Healing
isn't linear. Recovery isn't a destination you
arrive at and never leave.

But here's what's different:

I know my worth now. Not the worth that's measured by someone else's approval or validation. Not the worth that's contingent on being believed or supported or protected. But the inherent, unshakeable worth that comes from being human. From being alive. From being me.

I know my power now. The power to create. The power to transform. The power to turn pain into art, trauma into testimony, wounds into wisdom. The power to choose myself. The power to set boundaries. The power to say no. The power to say "I believe me" even when no one else does.

I know my truth now. And I no longer need anyone else to validate it. The truth exists whether it's acknowledged or not. The violation happened whether it's believed or not. My experience is real whether it's honored or not.

I don't need external validation because I have internal knowing.

I know my voice now. It took years to find it. Years of silence. Years of art speaking when words wouldn't come. Years of small, scared whispers before I could manage full volume. But now? Now I can scream if I need to. Now I can speak truth to power. Now I can say "this happened to me" without apologizing or softening or making it digestible for others' comfort.

I know my fire now. I understand it. I control it. I wield it intentionally. I know when to let it rage and when to let it simmer. I know how to use it to forge new paths instead of burning bridges. I know how to share its warmth with others who are cold with their own trauma. I know how to let it light the way for those still stumbling through darkness.

Part VII: The Gallery of Our Collective Survival

My painting hung in that school gallery. It was one piece, one story, one person's attempt to make sense of the unspeakable.

But I wasn't the only one painting pain into beauty.

I wasn't the only one transforming trauma into art.

I wasn't the only one screaming silently through creative expression.

There is a whole gallery of us. Survivors who found our voices through music, through writing, through dance, through visual art, through activism, through simply continuing to exist and refusing to be erased.

We are the artists of our own recovery.

We are the authors of our own narratives.

We are the curators of our own healing.

And together, we create something bigger than our individual stories. We create a collective testimony. We create a movement. We create space for others to speak their truths. We create a world where silence is no longer the default response to violence.

Every survivor who speaks up makes it easier for the next one.

Every person who refuses to be silenced weakens the systems that rely on our silence.

Every voice that says "me too" reminds another survivor they're not alone.

This is how we change things. Not by being perfect victims who follow some prescribed healing timeline. Not by performing forgiveness for others' comfort. Not by making our trauma palatable or our pain digestible.

But by being real. By being honest. By being complicated and messy and angry and healing and broken and whole all at the same time.

By painting our fires and hanging them in galleries for others to see.

By saying "this happened to me, and I'm still here."

By transforming our silence into testimony.

By turning our wounds into wisdom.

By reclaiming what was taken.

Part VIII: The Fire You Give Others

Ms. Reyes saw something in my anger. She saw the raw power of it. She gave me permission to use it, to channel it, to transform it.

Now I see that same anger in others. I recognize it because I carried it. I know its weight, its heat, its potential for both destruction and creation.

And I do for them what Ms. Reyes did for me: I see it. I name it. I give them permission to use it.

Your anger is not ugly. It's honest.

Your pain is not weakness. It's evidence that you survived something that should have destroyed you.

Your scars are not shameful. They're proof of your strength.

Your story is not a burden. It's a testimony.

Your voice is not too much. It's exactly what someone else needs to hear to find their own.

Your fire is not dangerous. It's sacred.

Use it.

Paint it. Write it. Sing it. Dance it. Speak it. Live it.

Let it burn away everything that no longer serves you—the shame that was never yours, the silence that protected your abuser, the smallness you adopted to make others comfortable, the performance of being "over it" when healing is still happening.

Let it forge something new—boundaries that protect you, strength that sustains you, wisdom that guides you, compassion that connects you to others who understand, power that allows you to not just survive but to thrive.

Let it light the way for others—the ones still stumbling through their darkness, the ones who haven't found their voice yet, the ones who think they're alone, the ones who need to see that survival is possible, that transformation is real, that fire can create as powerfully as it destroys.

Part IX: The Mirror Now

I look in the mirror now—same chipped glass, different reflection.

I see a survivor. Not defined by what happened, but shaped by how I chose to respond to it.

I see an artist. Not despite the trauma, but because of how I chose to transform it.

I see a fighter. Not the kind that destroys everything in her path, but the kind that protects what matters and lets go of what doesn't.

I see a woman who reclaimed her innocence, not by pretending nothing happened, but by refusing to carry shame for someone else's violence.

I see a woman who reclaimed her anger, not by suppressing it, but by channeling it into something that creates rather than destroys.

I see a woman who reclaimed her voice, not by speaking perfectly, but by speaking truthfully.

I see a woman who reclaimed her body, not by forgetting what was done to it, but by remembering it belongs to her.

I see a woman who reclaimed her story, not by making it pretty, but by making it hers.

I see a woman who reclaimed her worth, not by earning it through achievement or validation, but by recognizing it was always there, unshakeable and inherent.

I see myself. Finally.

Not the stranger. Not the victim. Not the damaged goods. Not the attention-seeker. Not the liar.

Myself.

Complicated. Contradictory. Still healing. Still angry sometimes. Still triggered occasionally. Still carrying the weight. But also strong. Also creative. Also powerful. Also worthy. Also whole.

The viper is still there. It probably always will be. Trauma doesn't just disappear. But I've learned to live with it. I've learned that healing isn't about being "fixed" or "cured" or "back to normal." Healing is about integration. It's about carrying your story while refusing to let it carry you.

The fire is still there too. It probably always will be. But now it's mine. I control it. I direct it. I use it to create light instead of just heat. I use it to warm those who are cold with their own trauma instead of burning everyone in my path.

Part X: The Invitation

This is my story. But it's also your invitation.

If you've been silent, speak.

If you've been small, expand.

If you've been ashamed, reclaim.

If you've been dismissed, declare.

If you've been carrying someone else's shame, put it down.

If you've been living in someone else's narrative, write your own.

If you've been suppressing your anger, use it.

If you've been dimming your fire, let it burn.

You don't need permission. You don't need validation. You don't need anyone to believe you to know your own truth. You don't need to wait until you're "healed enough" to speak. You don't need to make your story digestible or your pain palatable or your anger acceptable.

You just need to start.

Paint your fire. Write your truth. Sing your story. Dance your healing. Speak your testimony.

Do it messy. Do it imperfect. Do it scared. Do it angry. Do it while you're still figuring it out.

Just do it.

Because somewhere, someone is waiting to see your painting in the gallery. Someone is waiting to hear that they're not alone. Someone is waiting for permission to use their anger. Someone is waiting to see that survival is possible.

Someone is waiting for you to go first.

So go.

From silence to fire to self-worth—this is the path of reclamation.

And you are invited to walk it.

I was a stranger in my own mirror. Now I am the one looking back.

I was silent. Now I am fire.

I was violated. Now I am whole.

I was not believed. Now I believe myself.

I was told I was attention-seeking. Now I demand attention because my story matters.

I was a victim. Now I am a survivor. Tomorrow, I'll be a thriver.

This is my reclamation. What's yours?

To every survivor reading this: I see you. I believe you. Your anger is valid. Your pain is real. Your healing is yours. Your story matters. Your voice deserves to be heard. You are not alone.

From silence to fire to self-worth—may you find your way home to yourself.

May you reclaim everything that was taken.

May you discover that you were never broken, just breaking free.

May your fire burn bright.

Mixed Personalities: The Many Faces of Me

Introduction: The Multiplicity of Self

Identity is not a monolith. It's not one static thing you discover at eighteen and carry unchanged through life. Identity is fluid, fractured, faceted—a prism catching different lights depending on the angle, the environment, the need of the moment.

Some people call it code-switching. Some call it adaptation. Some call it survival. I call it truth.

Because the truth is, I am not one person. I am many. And each version of me—each persona, each alter ego, each carefully constructed identity—exists for a reason. Born from necessity, shaped by experience, wielded with intention.

Let me introduce you to the women who live inside me. The ones who emerge when Taria needs backup, when the situation requires a different energy, when being myself means being multiple selves. These aren't masks I wear—they're dimensions of who I am. Each one as real, as valid, as necessary as the others.

Think of them as my inner council, my personal Avengers, my board of directors. Each with their own origin story, their own superpowers, their own purpose. Together, they make me whole. Separately, they make me dynamic.

Welcome to the multiplicity of me.

ALEXIS KERRINGTON

Name: Alexis Kerrington
Date of Birth: 2019
Place of Birth: South Chicago Suburbs
Named After: Alexis Carrington from "Dynasty" (the deceitful mother who was almost murdered)

CERTIFICATE OF PERSONA

This is to certify that on an undisclosed night in 2019, in response to environmental threat and social anxiety, there was born:

ALEXIS KERRINGTON

Primary Function: Internal Savior, Reality Escape Artist, Environmental Shield
Physical Presentation: Fiery redhead (the color of warning and warmth)
Behavioral Characteristics: Socially adept surface, deeply complex interior; navigates uneasy environments with practiced ease
Special Abilities: Instant alias generation, threat assessment, social deflection, protective presence
Activation Triggers: Persistent unwanted attention, uncomfortable social situations, instinctive danger signals, need for anonymity
Duration of Service: 5+ years and counting

THE ORIGIN STORY

Alexis was born on a night that should have been fun. A party. Music. People. The kind of environment where you're supposed to let loose, be yourself, relax.

But then there was him. The persistent guy. The one who wouldn't take a hint. The one whose attention felt less like flattery and more like surveillance. The one who kept asking for her number, kept pushing, kept hovering.

Instincts kicked in. Not panic—something more primal. An internal alarm system that said: *You need to be someone else right now. You need distance. You need protection.*

And just like that, Alexis was born.

She gave him a name that wasn't mine. Created a persona on the spot. A shield made of smoke and mirrors and fiery red hair that said "I'm interesting" while also saying "you don't really know me."

WHO SHE IS

Alexis Kerrington is an interesting one. Her name carries the weight of television drama—deceitful, almost murdered, surviving against the odds. But my Alexis is different from her namesake. She's not deceitful for manipulation's sake. She's protective. Strategic. A guardian at the gate of my authentic self.

Alexis, with her fiery red hair, stands out in any crowd. Her presence is both comforting and mysterious, like a flickering flame in the dark. She navigates social settings with ease—or at least it seems that way. The performance is flawless. The smile is practiced. The small talk flows effortlessly.

But it's when she's alone that her true essence shines through, illuminating the depths of her complexity. Because Alexis isn't just a party trick or a throwaway alias. She's a fully realized persona, complete with her own energy, her own way of moving through the world, her own purpose.

She serves as a shield when environments seem uneasy. When the vibe is off. When someone's attention feels predatory rather than friendly. When I need to be present in a space without being vulnerable in that space.

Alexis has been my default for five years and still upholds what she was created to serve: **protection through misdirection, safety through strategic identity**.

WHEN ALEXIS EMERGES

- At parties where I don't know everyone
- When strangers ask too many personal questions
- In situations where being "Taria" feels too exposed
- When someone's energy reads as unsafe
- During first dates with people I'm not sure about yet
- In professional networking events where I need distance
- Anywhere my gut says "be careful"

WHAT ALEXIS TAUGHT ME

That it's okay to have boundaries that look like other identities. That protection doesn't always mean physical distance—sometimes it means identity distance. That there's power in choosing what parts of yourself you share and when. That survival sometimes requires creativity.

Alexis is my reminder that I don't owe anyone access to my authentic self, especially not when that access might compromise my safety.

YVETTE FITCH

Name: Yvette Fitch
Date of Birth: 2020
Place of Birth: Denison University
Named After: Classic, timeless femininity with an edge

CERTIFICATE OF PERSONA

This is to certify that during the progressive yet still-repressed era of 2020, in response to sexual awakening and societal judgment, there was born:

YVETTE FITCH

Primary Function: Sexual Liberation Advocate, Desire Expresser, Norm Challenger
Physical Presentation: Unapologetically sensual, confidently provocative
Behavioral Characteristics: Sexually curious and expressive, boundary-pusher, unashamed
Special Abilities: Fearless flirtation, authentic desire expression, judgment resistance, bisexual pride
Activation Triggers: Sexual topics, attraction moments, queer spaces, judgment about body counts

or clothing choices

Core Philosophy: "I go for what I want and don't hide my interest in men or women"

THE ORIGIN STORY

Yvette was born during a time when talking about sex in public was not necessarily taboo, given the progressive era, but still tiptoed around. Everyone wanted to seem sex-positive, but nobody wanted to actually talk about sex honestly. Everyone claimed to support sexual liberation, but judgment still lurked beneath the surface.

I was tired of the performance. Tired of pretending I wasn't interested when I was. Tired of playing coy. Tired of the ridiculous rules about who could express desire and how and when. Tired of the double standards—men celebrated for sexual confidence, women shamed for the same.

So Yvette emerged. A force to be reckoned with. A sexually liberated beast who refuses to apologize for her appetites.

WHO SHE IS

Yvette is unapologetically herself. Despite being labeled with derogatory terms such as "hoe" or "thot", she refuses to conform to societal expectations. Those words don't wound her—they bounce off like water off wax. Because Yvette knows that those labels say more about the people using them than they do about her.

Yvette has never been what her generation likes to call "easy," but she goes for what she wants and does not hide her interest in men or women. There's a difference between being "easy" and being honest. Between being "slutty" and being sexually autonomous. Between being "desperate" and being clear about desire.

Yvette navigates her evolving sexual identity with boldness, embracing desires without inhibition. She's still learning, still exploring, still asking questions. Bisexuality is a journey, not a destination, and Yvette walks that path with her head held high.

Despite occasional scrutiny from the lesbian community about being "fake gay," she still celebrates from June 1st to the 30th with no fucks given. (And honestly? The fact that queer people police each other's queerness is exhausting. Yvette doesn't have time for that nonsense.)

Yvette is still learning her sexual self, constantly asking questions that get her judged and profiled. Questions like:

- Why do people care who I share my body with?
- Why do body counts matter?
- Why is speaking about sex in social environments looked down upon?
- Why does showing more skin mean you're a provocative whore?

These aren't rhetorical questions for Yvette. She genuinely wants to understand the logic behind sexual shame. She wants someone to explain why women's sexuality is simultaneously commodified and condemned. She wants to know why the same society that profits from sex work, porn, and sexual imagery also punishes women for being sexual beings.

Nobody's given her good answers yet.

Yvette exudes confidence in her sexuality, unapologetically embracing every facet of her desires. Her presence is electrifying, sparking conversations and challenging societal norms. She moves through life with a boldness that captivates those around her, leaving a trail of curiosity and admiration in her wake.

WHEN YVETTE EMERGES

- During conversations about sex and sexuality
- When someone tries to shame me for my choices
- In queer spaces where I want to be fully myself
- When I'm attracted to someone and want to express it
- During Pride month (all 30 days, thank you very much)
- When someone asks about my "body count" like it matters
- Anytime I'm tired of performing purity

WHAT YVETTE TAUGHT ME

That sexual autonomy is revolutionary. That expressing desire is not the same as being desperate. That bisexuality is valid even when people question it. That my body, my choices—period. That the rules around women's sexuality are designed to control us, not protect us. That there's nothing wrong with wanting what you want and saying so.

Yvette is my reminder that I don't owe anyone sexual modesty, explanations about my sexuality, or apologies for my desires.

LORETTA HENRY

Name: Loretta Henry
Date of Birth: 2020
Place of Birth: Denison University
Named After: Old soul wisdom and gossipy grandmas everywhere

CERTIFICATE OF PERSONA

This is to certify that as a humorous nod to acceptance and ancestral wisdom, there was born:

LORETTA HENRY

Primary Function: Wisdom Keeper, Life Experience Sharer, Neighborhood Grandma
Physical Presentation: Old soul energy in a young body
Behavioral Characteristics: Nosey as hell, jovial, oversharing, boundary-challenged, kind-hearted

Special Abilities: Life advice dispensing, story-telling, truth-speaking (sometimes too much truth), alcohol-activated sociability

Activation Triggers: Being under the influence, someone needing advice, gossip opportunities, community gathering

Self-Description: "The grandma who bakes and feeds the entire neighborhood while knowing everyone and enough about them"

THE ORIGIN STORY

Miss Loretta Henry is an old soul by nature and name. She is wise and nosey as hell.

Loretta was born as a humorous nod to acceptance—acceptance of the gossipy, oversharing, too-much-information parts of myself that society says are inappropriate. The parts that want to tell you my whole life story within five minutes of meeting you. The parts that ask intrusive questions because I'm genuinely curious. The parts that can't keep a secret to save my life (not the important ones, but the juicy ones? Gone).

She embodies the spirit of her gossipy lineage. Every family has that auntie or grandma who knows everybody's business and isn't shy about sharing it. Loretta is that energy bottled up and given form.

WHO SHE IS

Loretta is always lurking around silently (or not so silently, if we're being honest). She's the one listening to conversations at the next table, filing away information, connecting dots. But she really comes out to party when she's under the influence. Alcohol is like Loretta's activation code—two drinks in, and she's introducing herself to everyone, even people who've met her multiple times before.

"Hi, I'm Loretta! Have I told you about the time when..."

She introduces herself every time, even around those who have met her before, because in Loretta's mind, every encounter is a fresh start, a new opportunity to connect and share.

Loretta is pretty open about her life experiences and is always willing to share words of power/wisdom/assistance, whatever one may require. Need advice about relationships? Loretta's got stories. Wondering about a career decision? Loretta knows someone who knows someone. Struggling with family drama? Oh honey, let Loretta tell you about drama.

Loretta's jovial demeanor and penchant for sharing life experiences make her a cherished confidante. People love Loretta—she's warm, she's real, she makes you feel like you've known her for years even if you just met.

But in regard to her intrusive nature, she lacks boundaries and struggles to refrain from disclosing sensitive information without consent, which can often be problematic for her. Loretta will ask you about your dating life at Thanksgiving dinner. Loretta will tell your business to someone who definitely didn't need to know. Loretta means well, but sometimes her nosiness and her oversharing get her (and me) in trouble.

Loretta describes herself as the grandma who bakes and feeds the entire neighborhood while knowing everyone and enough about them. She wants to nurture you with food and life advice in equal measure. She wants to know your story so she can properly care for you.

Loretta's presence is like a comforting blanket, wrapping those around her in warmth and familiarity. She effortlessly weaves in and out of conversations, offering sage advice and a listening ear to anyone in need. Despite her tendency to overstep boundaries, her intentions are always rooted in kindness and a genuine desire to connect with others.

WHEN LORETTA EMERGES

- After a couple drinks at social gatherings
- When someone needs life advice
- During family functions
- When there's good gossip to share (or extract)
- In moments of deep conversation
- When I'm feeling particularly nurturing
- Anytime someone says "I need to tell you something"

WHAT LORETTA TAUGHT ME

That vulnerability and oversharing, while sometimes problematic, come from a place of wanting connection. That wisdom doesn't always look polished—sometimes it looks like your drunk auntie telling you real talk at 2am. That boundaries are important, but so is radical honesty. That people often need someone to listen more than they need someone with perfect advice.

Loretta is my reminder that connection requires vulnerability, even if that vulnerability sometimes looks messy.

LONDON FITCH

Name: London Fitch
Date of Birth: Spring Break 2022
Place of Birth: South Chicago Suburbs
Named After: Transformation, rebirth, and global sophistication

CERTIFICATE OF PERSONA

This is to certify that during a time of confusion, pain, grief, and hope in Spring 2022, there was born:

LONDON FITCH

Primary Function: Symbol of Rebirth, Transformation Artist, Authentic Self Seeker
Physical Presentation: Ever-changing (orange finger waves, box braids, red or blonde pixie cut, bantu knots, natural twist out, head wraps tied in countless ways)

Behavioral Characteristics: Mood-dependent (quiet and reserved OR loud and outgoing), well-known, liked by many, feared by some

Special Abilities: Style transformation, mood adaptation, purposeful evolution, authentic expression (when she allows it)

Activation Triggers: Need for change, search for purpose, moments of self-discovery, creative expression

Core Fear: That her purpose is subject to change, that she'll never settle into one true self

THE ORIGIN STORY

London was born during a time of confusion, pain, grief, and hope. Spring Break 2022—a time that should have been about relaxation and fun, but instead became a crucible of transformation.

I was grieving who I'd been. Confused about who I was becoming. In pain from what I'd survived. Hopeful about who I could be.

Out of that mess, London emerged. A symbol of rebirth. The phoenix rising from ashes, but make it fashionable and perpetually evolving.

WHO SHE IS

London switches up her style constantly. Her hair could be in orange finger waves one week, box braids the next, a red or blonde pixie cut after that, bantu knots for a special occasion, a natural twist out for everyday, and most importantly, a head wrap tied in one of many ways—each style intentional, each look a statement, each transformation a declaration.

Her hair is her canvas, and she paints it with the colors and textures of her current state of mind. Orange for boldness. Red for passion. Blonde for reinvention. Natural for authenticity. Wrapped for protection and cultural pride.

London can be quiet and reserved, or she can be loud and outgoing, depending on her mood and environment. She doesn't believe in being one consistent thing. She adapts. She flows. She reads the room and decides who she needs to be in that moment.

Safe to say that London is well known, liked by many (as it appears), and feared by some. The "well known" part comes from her ever-changing aesthetic—people remember London because she's never the same twice. The "liked by many" part is surface-level; people appreciate her creativity and boldness. The "feared by some" part? That comes from the fact that London doesn't follow rules. She doesn't stay in boxes. She makes people uncomfortable with her refusal to be categorized.

London attempts to be unapologetically herself in all cases. Attempts being the key word. Because here's the truth: sometimes that is not the case and she bottles her authenticity in a cranberry juice glass bottle. Sometimes the pressure to be consistent, to pick a lane, to settle into one version of herself becomes too much. So she performs. She gives people what they expect. She bottles up the full truth of who she is and presents a more digestible version.

London is the kind of woman who is constantly changing and reworking herself to align with her purpose. A purpose that is subject to change—which is a fear of London. What if she never finds her "thing"? What if she's always becoming and never arriving? What if her superpower (transformation) is also her curse (inconsistency)?

London's essence is as fluid as the colors of her ever-changing hair. She embodies the spirit of transformation, embracing each new phase of her existence with grace and determination. Whether she's wrapped in a vibrant headscarf or sporting a daring shortcut, London's outward appearance reflects the evolution of her inner self. She moves through life with quiet confidence, leaving an indelible mark on everyone she encounters.

WHEN LONDON EMERGES

- During times of major life transition
- When I'm searching for purpose
- In creative moments
- When I need to reinvent myself
- During periods of growth and change
- When the old version of me no longer fits
- Anytime I'm trying to figure out who I'm becoming

WHAT LONDON TAUGHT ME

That transformation is not failure. That changing your mind, your style, your path doesn't mean you're lost—it means you're growing. That purpose doesn't have to be static. That evolution is beautiful even when it's confusing. That you can be many things and still be whole.

London is my reminder that I'm allowed to become, and become again, and keep becoming for as long as I live.

THE COLLECTIVE:
Understanding the Multiplicity

The fragmented personas of Alexis Kerrington, Yvette Fitch, Loretta Henry, and London collectively yield a tapestry of complexity and depth. Each alter ego embodies unique characteristics and experiences, reflecting the multifaceted nature of human identity.

From Alexis' fiery resilience to Yvette's unapologetic embrace of sexuality, from Loretta's wise counsel to London's fluidity of self-expression—these personas navigate the existence of life with courage and authenticity.

Together, they remind me that identity is not confined to a singular form, but rather exists in a kaleidoscope of perspectives and possibilities.

Why They Matter

Some people might read this and think I'm joking. Or that I have dissociative identity disorder. Or that I'm just being dramatic about normal human complexity.

But here's the thing: **whether or not people label me insane or respect my personas like Sasha Fierce or The Harajuku Barbie, these parts of me are real.**

Beyoncé has Sasha Fierce. Nicki Minaj has Roman Zolanski and the Harajuku Barbie. Artists have always understood what psychology is now confirming: we contain multitudes. We are not one-dimensional beings. We adapt, we transform, we become different versions of ourselves depending on context, need, and safety.

My personas aren't a disorder. They're a strategy. A survival mechanism. A creative expression. A way of honoring all the different parts of myself that emerge in different situations.

The Integration

The goal isn't to kill off these personas or to "integrate" them into one consistent Taria. The goal is to understand when each one emerges, why they're needed, and how to wield them intentionally rather than reactively.

Alexis protects me. Yvette liberates me. Loretta connects me. London transforms me.

I need all of them. They make me dynamic, adaptable, resilient, whole.

The Prayer

As I journey through the fragmented pieces of myself, I pray I continue to find peace in the diversity of my existence and embrace the beauty of my ever-evolving selves.

I pray I never feel pressured to collapse into one acceptable version of Taria.

I pray I honor each persona's purpose and wisdom.

I pray I use them strategically, not desperately.

I pray others understand that multiplicity is not madness—it's mastery.

The Invitation (Again)

Do you have personas? Names for the different versions of yourself that emerge in different contexts?

The you who shows up at work versus the you who shows up at home?

The you who parties versus the you who reflects?

The you who's bold versus the you who's careful?

The you who's sexual versus the you who's professional?

Maybe you've never named them. Maybe you've never thought about them as separate entities. Maybe you just experience them as mood shifts or context-dependent behavior.

But what if you gave them names? What if you wrote their birth certificates? What if you understood their purposes?

What if you stopped seeing your multiplicity as inconsistency and started seeing it as adaptability?

What if you stopped judging yourself for being "different people in different situations" and started celebrating your range?

What if your many selves are not a problem to solve but a superpower to harness?

I am Taria. I am also Alexis, Yvette, Loretta, and London.

I am one. I am many.

I am consistent in my multiplicity.

I am whole in my fragments.

And so are you.

Birth Certificate: Human Being
Date of Birth: The moment you realized you contain multitudes
Primary Function: To be authentically, dynamically, unapologetically yourself—all versions
Special Ability: The courage to honor your complexity

Threads: Mini Poems on Finding Freedom

The Geography of Peace

Freedom isn't always found in grand gestures or revolutionary moments. Sometimes freedom lives in the familiar—in the street you grew up on, in the friends who see you fully, in the driver's seat of your first car.

I am free in experiences of freedom. My hometown, my home on the hill, and my first big girl purchase are some of many. Each poem below takes you on an adventurous introduction to who and what they are, and most importantly the power it grasps in my mind and body.

These are my sanctuaries. The places—physical and emotional—where I can exhale. Where I can be all of me without translation or performance. Where the world's weight lifts, even if just for a moment.

The first poem, **Country Aire, Markham IL**, named after a small town, evokes the nostalgic feeling and location of my hometown—the foundation of who I am, the cultural roots that ground me.

The second poem, **Home on the Hill**, captures the essence of finding freedom in friendship—the chosen family that holds you when you're far from home.

The third poem, **Bug Fitch**, is about my most precious and prized possession, my sanctuary on wheels—the mobile space where I can be completely myself.

During the brainstorming phase, these three topics came to mind and instead of writing about one, a short poem for each will do.

These are my threads. The connections that weave through my life, stitching together past and present, roots and growth, solitude and community.

Enjoy.

Country Aire, Markham IL

A love letter to the place that made me

In the days of sunlit youth, a dance of nostalgia,
Where norms were stitched in respect's golden fabric.
Entering rooms, a ritual of honor, a gentle nod,
Whispers of "hello" to elders, a symphony of regard.

Old-school R&B crooning through the air,
A soulful soundtrack, memories we wear.
Sunday mornings, a sacred sweep of time,
Mickey Mouse pancakes, a playful chime.

Children and elders, at the table, first,
A banquet of bonds, where love would burst.
Family BBQs, smoke swirling high,
Box braids, cornrows, under the sunlit sky.

Tight coils, brown gel, and headwraps so grand,
Expressions of self, stories in each strand.
Unique names, echoes of heritage strong,
In the rhythm of belonging, where we all belong.

Home by street lights, a curfew's embrace,
Candy stores whispering childhood grace.
The Icee man's melody, a sweet, cool call,
Juke jams and slang, memories enthrall.

Summers at Grandma's, an eternal embrace,
Roasting friends, nicknames, laughter's grace.
A tapestry woven with love, each thread,
In the fabric of culture, where memories are bred.

Reflection: What Country Aire Means

Country Aire, Markham IL—it's more than a location. It's a feeling. It's the muscle memory of respect and ritual. It's knowing that when you walk into a room with elders, you speak first. You acknowledge. You honor.

It's the soundtrack of my childhood: old-school R&B floating through open windows on summer days, the kind of music that made you feel connected to something bigger than yourself, to a lineage of soul and struggle and survival and joy.

It's Sunday mornings that felt sacred not because of church (though there was that too), but because of the ritual. The pancakes shaped like Mickey Mouse, made with love by hands that had made them a thousand times before. The gathering at the table where children and elders ate first—not because they were most important, but because feeding the young and honoring the old was how we showed love.

It's family BBQs where the smoke rose like prayers and the laughter was loud and the music was louder. Where aunties stood with one hand on their hip and a plate in the other, telling stories that got embellished with each retelling. Where uncles manned the grill like it was their kingdom. Where cousins ran wild until the streetlights came on.

It's the pride in our hair—box braids that took hours, cornrows that were works of art, tight coils slicked down with brown gel, headwraps tied with intention and cultural memory. Each style a story, each strand an expression of self in a world that often told us our natural beauty wasn't enough.

It's the names we carried—unique, meaningful, echoing heritage strong. Not "easy" names. Not names designed for white teachers' comfort. Names that announced: we are here, we are proud, we belong to a legacy.

It's home by street lights. That universal Black childhood experience where you knew exactly how much daylight you had left, where the amber glow of streetlights meant your mama was about to call your full government name if you weren't inside in the next five minutes.

It's the candy store that knew us all by name. The Icee man whose melody announced his arrival blocks away, and we'd scramble for change, running barefoot through summer grass to catch him before he turned the corner.

It's juke jams where the music was explicit and the dancing was expressive and we learned early that Black joy is resistance, that our culture is rich, that we don't need permission to celebrate ourselves.

It's summers at Grandma's house—the headquarters of family, the place where everyone gathered, where love was measured in plates piled high and criticism delivered with a laugh and wisdom dropped casually between card games.

It's roasting your friends because that's how you showed love. It's nicknames that stuck for life. It's laughter that came from the belly and bonds that felt unbreakable.

Country Aire, Markham IL is where I learned to be Black and proud. Where I learned that our culture is beautiful. Where I learned respect and community and joy in the midst of struggle. Where I learned that home isn't just a place—it's a feeling, a set of values, a way of being in the world.

This is my root. This is my foundation. This is where freedom first felt like belonging.

Home on the Hill

A love letter to the friendships that saved me

On this hill, far enough from my roots, I stand,
A product of a community left behind.
Yet, in this vast land,
I find freedom in the friends I've mined.

None-judging souls who stand by my side,
Wiping away tears, patting my back.
In ceremonies, they are my pride,
Unwavering support, no love they lack.

They brave discomfort to be my friend,
Showing up without a plea.

In solitude, no judgments they send,
Correcting me with love, setting my spirit free.

Among the friends, a sanctuary I've found,
Caring for my mental health, they inquire.
Extensions and absences, understanding abound,
In their accountability, true virtues transpire.

Open doors and open hearts they share,
A policy of support, a haven for me.
Distinguishing between a listening ear and
despair,
They speak highly of me in rooms where I cannot
be.

On this hill, away from my past,
I discover freedom in friendship's embrace,
A testament to bonds that forever last,
I find solace in this unfamiliar space.

Reflection: What Home on the Hill Means

Denison University sits on a hill—literally and metaphorically. It's far from Markham, far from Country Aire, far from everything I knew. It's a predominantly white institution in a small Ohio town where I am often one of few, one of the only, the representative of an entire community I never asked to represent.

It should have been isolating. It could have been lonely. The distance from home, the culture shock, the code-switching required to navigate spaces that weren't built for me—all of it could have broken me.

But instead, I found freedom. Not freedom from struggle (that's still there), but freedom in friendship. Freedom in finding my people on this hill far from home.

These friends—they're not from my neighborhood. They don't all share my background. Some of them had never met a Black person before meeting me (which, yes, is wild in 2025, but that's America). Some of them are still learning, still growing, still making mistakes and doing better.

But what they all have in common is this: they show up.

They are none-judging souls who stand by my side. When I'm falling apart, when the weight of being "the only one" gets too heavy, when the microaggressions pile up, when I'm homesick or heartsick or just sick of performing—they're there. Wiping away tears. Patting my back. Not trying to fix it, just being present.

In ceremonies, they are my pride. When I walk across stages, when I receive recognition, when I'm honored for my work—they're in the audience, loud and proud, cheering like I'm family. Because I am. Chosen family.

Unwavering support, no love they lack. This line hits different because it's true. They don't just support me when it's convenient or comfortable. They brave discomfort to be my friend. They show up to conversations about race even when it's awkward. They check their friends when someone says something ignorant. They use their privilege to amplify my voice, not speak over it.

They show up without a plea. I don't have to beg for their presence. I don't have to convince them I'm worthy of friendship. They just... show up. Consistently. Reliably. Without expecting anything in return.

In solitude, no judgments they send. When I need space, when I cancel plans, when I go ghost because I'm processing trauma or dealing with family stuff or just need to be alone—they don't take it personally. They don't guilt trip. They just say "I'm here when you're ready."

They correct me with love, setting my spirit free. Real friends don't just hype you up—they call you in when you're wrong. They hold you accountable. But they do it with love, not judgment. With the intention of helping you grow, not tearing you down.

Among these friends, a sanctuary I've found. The kind where I can talk about my mental health without shame. Where I can say "I'm not okay" and not have to perform strength. Where I can be vulnerable and messy and imperfect and still be loved.

They care for my mental health, they inquire. Not in a performative "how are you?" way, but genuinely. They notice when I'm off. They ask follow-up questions. They remember what I told them last week and check in.

Extensions and absences, understanding abound. When I need deadline extensions because trauma doesn't care about due dates. When I miss events because my social battery is drained. When I can't show up because I'm dealing with stuff I can't talk about yet—they understand. They advocate for me. They cover for me. They hold space for my humanity.

In their accountability, true virtues transpire. They hold themselves accountable for learning, growing, being better friends. They don't expect me to educate them about everything, but they also don't pretend racism doesn't exist. They walk that line with intention.

Open doors and open hearts they share. Their homes are my homes. Their families become my families away from home. Their resources become shared resources. There's no scarcity mindset—just abundance, generosity, love.

A policy of support, a haven for me. It's not just reactive support when crisis hits—it's a standing policy. A guarantee. A covenant of friendship that says "I've got you, always."

Distinguishing between a listening ear and despair. They know when I need to vent versus when I need intervention. They don't minimize my pain by trying to fix everything, but they also don't let me drown. They know the difference between being a listening ear and watching someone spiral into despair—and they respond accordingly.

They speak highly of me in rooms where I cannot be. This is the one that gets me. Because I'll never know all the times they defended me, advocated for me, hyped me up, corrected misconceptions about me. But I know they do. Because that's what real friends do—they protect your name when you're not there to protect it yourself.

On this hill, away from my past, I discover freedom in friendship's embrace. Not freedom from my roots (those are essential), but freedom to grow beyond them. Freedom to be all of myself—the Country Aire girl and the college student, the cultural product and the individual, the representative and the person.

A testament to bonds that forever last. These friendships aren't just college friendships that'll fade after graduation. These are life friendships. Soul friendships. The kind that survive distance and time and life changes.

I find solace in this unfamiliar space. The hill isn't home in the way Markham is home. But it's home in a different way. It's the home I chose. The family I built. The sanctuary I created.

This is my chosen home. This is my found family. This is where freedom feels like unconditional love.

Bug Fitch

A love letter to my sanctuary on wheels

Bug, my faithful sweetpea of grey,
A minivan they mocked, yet my haven, my stay.
Reliable companion through trials and glee,
In your spacious embrace, I find solace free.

Your form may be simple, your butt quite grand,
But within your walls, I find peace firsthand.
A canvas of color adorns your interior,
Flowers, succulents, rhinestones, their stories are superior.

For hours, I linger within your domain,
Crying, screaming, or singing, free from restraint.
You witness my joys, my sorrows, my strife,
In your embrace, I carve moments of life.

You were my first big girl purchase, Bug, my dear,
A symbol of independence, devoid of fear.

Through journeys long and moments still,
You're more than a car, you're my sanctuary, my fill.

Reflection: What Bug Fitch Means

Bug Fitch. My grey minivan. My most precious and prized possession. The vehicle that people mock ("Really? A minivan?") but that I love with my whole heart.

Bug, my faithful sweetpea of grey—she's not flashy. She's not the car I dreamed about as a kid. She's not turning heads on the highway or getting compliments at stoplights. She's practical, reliable, spacious, and yes, her butt is quite grand (that rear end is ROBUST, okay?).

But Bug is mine. The first major purchase I made with my own money. The first vehicle I chose for myself, not what someone else thought I should have. The first space that was entirely, completely, unarguably mine.

A minivan they mocked, yet my haven, my stay. People love to joke about minivans. "Soccer mom vibes." "Where are your three kids?" "Having a midlife crisis early?" Let them laugh. They don't understand. Bug isn't just transportation—she's transformation. She's therapy. She's sanctuary.

Reliable companion through trials and glee. Bug has been there through everything. The drive back to campus after traumatic spring break. The late-night crying sessions in parking lots when I couldn't cry in my dorm. The road trips with friends where we sang too loud and laughed until our stomachs hurt. The solo drives when I needed to think, to process, to just be.

In your spacious embrace, I find solace free. That space—that's what matters. Enough room to stretch out. To recline the seat all the way back and stare at the ceiling. To curl up in the back when I need to feel held. To fill with friends and music and possibility.

Your form may be simple, your butt quite grand, but within your walls, I find peace firsthand. Bug isn't about external appearance—she's about internal experience. Inside her, I'm safe. Inside her, I'm free. Inside her, I'm home.

A canvas of color adorns your interior. I decorated Bug like I'd decorate an apartment. Flowers hanging from the rearview mirror. Succulents in the cup holders (fake ones, because I can't keep real plants alive even in ideal conditions, let alone a car). Rhinestones on the dashboard catching sunlight. Each decoration intentional, each addition a way of making this space mine.

Flowers, succulents, rhinestones, their stories are superior. Every decoration has a story. The flower from the festival where I felt free. The succulent that reminds me to care for myself. The rhinestones that catch light and remind me I can sparkle even in darkness.

For hours, I linger within your domain. Bug is where I go when I need to disappear without leaving. When my dorm feels too public. When home feels too far. When I need solitude but can't stand stillness. I sit in Bug for hours. Sometimes parked at scenic overlooks. Sometimes in random parking lots. Sometimes just in the driveway.

Crying, screaming, or singing, free from restraint. Bug has heard it all. The ugly crying when grief hits. The screaming when anger needs release. The singing at the top of my lungs when joy demands expression. The prayers when I need to talk to something bigger than myself. The silence when words won't come.

You witness my joys, my sorrows, my strife. Bug holds all of it. The celebrations and the breakdowns. The epiphanies and the existential crises. The laughter and the tears. Bug is the witness to my full humanity—no performance, no filter, no code-switching.

In your embrace, I carve moments of life. Life happens in Bug. Real, unfiltered, messy, beautiful life. Conversations that change everything. Realizations that shift perspective. Moments of peace that feel like coming home to myself.

You were my first big girl purchase, Bug, my dear. This line is everything. Because Bug represents more than transportation—she represents independence. Agency. The ability to leave when I need to. The freedom to go where I want, when I want. The power to have space that's mine, that I control, that I paid for with my own money.

A symbol of independence, devoid of fear. Buying Bug was scary. It was a big financial commitment. It was adulting in a real, tangible way. But it was also empowering. It was me saying "I can take care of myself. I can make big decisions. I can invest in my own freedom."

Through journeys long and moments still. Bug has taken me on road trips to places I'd never been. And she's held me in parking lots where I sat perfectly still, just breathing. Both matter. Movement and stillness. Journey and pause.

You're more than a car, you're my sanctuary, my fill. Bug fills me up when the world drains me. She's where I go to refill my cup, to remember who I am, to reconnect with myself. She's not just a vehicle— she's a vessel. A container for my fullest self.

This is my mobile sanctuary. This is my independence. This is where freedom feels like solitude and safety.

The Thread That Connects Them All

Country Aire taught me where I come from.

Home on the Hill taught me where I'm going.

Bug teaches me that I carry home with me, wherever I go.

These three spaces—the hometown that made me, the chosen community that holds me, the personal sanctuary that's always mine—they're all connected. They're all essential. They're all threads in the tapestry of my freedom.

I am free in experiences of freedom. Not just one kind of freedom, but multiple. Not just one place of peace, but many. Not just one definition of home, but several.

Freedom is my roots.
The cultural foundation, the community values, the respect and ritual of Country Aire.

Freedom is my branches.
The chosen family, the friendships that stretch me and support me, the Home on the Hill.

Freedom is my ability to move between them.
The independence, the sanctuary on wheels, the Bug that carries me between past and present, roots and growth, home and adventure.

Together, these three poems tell the story of a Black woman finding freedom in a world that often denies it. Finding peace in spaces she creates and communities she builds. Finding home not in one place, but in the thread that connects them all: **the**

unwavering knowledge that she belongs to herself.

Your Turn: Where Are Your Threads?

Where do you find freedom?

Not the abstract concept of freedom, but the tangible, visceral experience of it. Where do you feel at peace? Where can you exhale? Where do you belong so fully that you don't have to explain or perform or translate?

Is it a place from your childhood? A friend's house? Your car? A park? A coffee shop? Your bedroom? A city you visited once and never forgot?

Write about it. Paint it. Photograph it. Sing about it. However you express yourself, express this: **the geography of your peace.**

Because freedom isn't just political or philosophical. Freedom is personal. Freedom is the places and people and moments where you feel most like yourself.

Find your threads. Name them. Honor them. Return to them when the world feels too heavy.

They're not just places or people or possessions.

They're sanctuaries. They're freedom. They're home.

To Country Aire: Thank you for my roots.
To Home on the Hill: Thank you for my wings.
To Bug: Thank you for carrying me between them.

These are my threads. What are yours?

Hey Future Me: Black Women Rising in 2026

Original Letter - May 1, 2024

Hey Future Me, It's your girl, T, writing to you on a crisp May day in 2024. Can you believe it's already halfway through the year? Feels like just yesterday we were ringing in the new year, vowing for self-discovery and new beginnings. Let me tell you, these past few months haven't exactly been sunshine and rainbows, but hey, that's life, right?

Remember that grad school application that had our whole hearts in a chokehold? Yeah, that rejection sting still lingers a bit. But guess what? We didn't let it define us. We took that disappointment, that feeling of "not being good enough," and flipped the script. We devoured books on the topic, connected with professionals in the field, and even started chipping away at some online courses. Who knows, maybe that traditional path just wasn't meant to be, and something even greater awaits. Speaking of greater things, our career path might still be a winding road, but that's okay. We're exploring, trying new things, and most importantly, not letting fear hold us back. Remember that internship at that community organization you were nervous about applying for? Well, guess who got it? You did, girl! You're out there learning, gaining new skills, and maybe even discovering a hidden passion you never knew existed.

Now, let's talk about the real, raw stuff. Navigating this world as a Black woman can be a battle, honey. There will be days when the weight of societal expectations and the constant undercurrent of prejudice try to dim your light. But here's the thing: you're strong, beautiful, and worthy beyond measure. Remember all that self-reflection you did in the first few months? That inner work is building your resilience. You're learning to love yourself, flaws and all, and that's the most powerful weapon you can have in this fight. There's Larell, too. Things haven't been easy lately, a rollercoaster of good intentions and communication roadblocks. We're both growing, and changing, and sometimes that means growing apart. It's scary, this uncertainty, this wondering if "us" can weather the storm. But here's the thing, future me, remember how fiercely you believe in open communication and prioritizing your own happiness? I trust you made the right decision, whether that means staying by Larell's side and building something stronger together, or walking away with love and respect, knowing it was the best choice for you both. Either way, I can't wait to see where this chapter lands and what kind of love story unfolds in the years to come.

Most importantly, future me, never lose sight of your dreams. There will be bumps, detours, and moments of doubt, but don't let them derail you. Keep pushing forward, keep learning, and keep that fire for a better future burning bright. Remember, the world needs your unique voice, your strength, and your unapologetic Black excellence.

Can't wait to see what amazing things you've accomplished when I meet you again.

With love and fierce belief, TT Signed 05/01/24

Extended Reflection - October 2025

Hey Past Me,

It's me again, T, checking in from October 2025. Girl, if you could see where we are now. That letter you wrote in May 2024? I keep it saved on my phone, and I read it on the hard days when I need to remember how far we've come.

You were right about the traditional path not being for us. That grad school rejection? Best thing that could've happened. The work we did through that community internship opened doors we never saw coming. We're not just surviving anymore—we're building something real, something that matters. And yes, the career path is still winding, but now we know that's not a flaw in our journey. It's the journey itself.

But let me talk to you about what it means to be a Black woman in 2025, because past me, you need to hear this.

The battle you mentioned? It's still here. The weight is still heavy some days. We're watching our sisters navigate spaces that still weren't built for us, still fighting for seats at tables where our presence makes others uncomfortable, still code-switching and translating ourselves to survive in predominantly white institutions. The "strong Black woman" stereotype still tries to rob us of our right to be soft, to be vulnerable, to rest without guilt.

But something's shifting. We're done with the martyrdom. Black Women in 2025 are redefining what strength means—it's not about carrying the world on our shoulders while our own needs go unmet. It's about boundary-setting, about saying "no" without explanation, about choosing our peace over performance. We're unlearning the generational conditioning that told us we had to be twice as good to get half as much. We're learning that our worth isn't measured by our productivity or our ability to endure suffering with a smile.

The sisterhood is different now, too. We're building intentional communities, both online and in real life, where Black Women hold space for each other without judgment. Where we can talk about therapy, medication, rest, and pleasure without shame. Where we celebrate each other's wins without the scarcity mindset that told us there wasn't enough room for all of us to shine. We're mentoring each other, funding each other's dreams, and calling out the systems that pit us against one another.

Remember that self-reflection work you mentioned? That inner work became the foundation for everything. Therapy isn't a luxury anymore—it's survival. We're addressing the intergenerational trauma, the racial trauma, the ways we've internalized messages about our bodies, our hair, our skin, our voices. We're reclaiming joy as resistance. We're prioritizing pleasure and softness as revolutionary acts in a world that wants us exhausted and compliant.

And Larell? That chapter closed with grace. It hurt, past me. It hurt in ways you weren't ready for. But you did exactly what you said you would—you chose your happiness, you communicated honestly, and you walked away with love. The lesson wasn't about whether "us" could weather the storm. The lesson was that you are whole all by yourself, that partnership is a choice not a necessity, and that sometimes the greatest act of love is letting go.

What came after? Growth. Space. Time to figure out who T is when she's not performing for someone else's expectations. You're learning to date yourself first—taking yourself to museums, booking solo trips, investing in experiences that feed your soul. And yes, there's been new love interests, but now you approach them differently. You know your worth, you know your non-negotiables, and you're not shrinking yourself to fit into anyone's incomplete vision of who you should be.

Let me talk about the broader landscape for Black Women in 2025. We're seeing more of us in leadership positions, yes, but we're also seeing the cost of those positions. We're watching our sisters burn out, dealing with imposter syndrome, navigating microaggressions and the invisible labor of being "the only one" or "one of few" in rooms full of people who don't understand the weight we carry. We're having honest conversations about whether breaking glass ceilings is worth it if we're left bleeding from the shards.

But we're also creating our own tables. Black Women entrepreneurs are thriving, building businesses that serve our communities, creating generational wealth on our own terms. We're writing the books, creating the art, producing the films, designing the fashion, leading the movements. We're doing it with less funding, less support, less infrastructure—because that's what we've always done. But now we're also demanding better. We're calling out the inequities, the pay gaps, the lack of access to capital, the ways our labor and creativity are exploited.

Healthcare is still a battlefield. We're still fighting to be believed when we talk about our pain. We're still dying at disproportionate rates during childbirth. We're still watching our mothers and grandmothers struggle with conditions that could've been prevented if someone had just listened. But we're also becoming the doctors, the researchers, the advocates who are changing the system from within. We're creating our own wellness practices that honor our bodies, our histories, and our needs.

Politically, socially, economically—2025 is complex. We're navigating a world that simultaneously celebrates Black culture while devaluing Black lives. We're watching our contributions be commodified while our humanity is questioned. We're seeing the attacks on DEI initiatives, the rollback of protections, the attempts to erase our history from textbooks. But we're also organizing, mobilizing, and refusing to be silenced.

The mental health conversation in our community has exploded, and that's beautiful. We're talking about depression, anxiety, burnout, and trauma in ways our mothers and grandmothers couldn't. We're saying "I'm not okay" and finding that admission liberating rather than shameful. We're learning that rest is productive, that boundaries are healthy, that we don't have to be everyone's savior.

Here's what I wish I could tell you about being a Black woman in 2025: it's still hard, but we're getting better at not doing hard things alone. We're building networks of support. We're investing in our mental health. We're choosing ourselves without apology. We're celebrating our melanin, our curves, our hair in all its versatile glory—4C coils, locs, braids, wigs, whatever makes us feel powerful. We're rejecting the European beauty standards that never had space for us anyway.

We're also having tough conversations within our community—about colorism, about texturism, about the ways we sometimes perpetuate the very systems that oppress us. We're calling out misogynoir, the unique intersection of racism and sexism that targets Black Women specifically. We're demanding that Black men show up as allies, not just when it's convenient but consistently, especially when it costs them something.

Your dreams, past me? They're evolving. Some of the things you thought you wanted, you realized were conditioned desires—things you thought you should want because of what society valued. You're learning to dream bigger, wilder, more authentically. You're learning that your version of success doesn't have to look like anyone else's.

That fire for a better future you mentioned? It's still burning, but now it's more focused. You're learning that you can't save everyone, that you have to put on your own oxygen mask first. You're learning that revolution starts with self-preservation, that you can't dismantle oppressive systems if you're too exhausted to stand.

The world does need your unique voice, your strength, your unapologetic Black excellence—you were right about that. But it also needs your softness, your vulnerability, your right to just be. You don't have to be excellent all the time. You don't have to be strong all the time. You get to be human, messy, imperfect, and still completely worthy of love, respect, and all the good things life has to offer.

To all the Black Women reading this in 2025: we're still here, still rising, still creating magic out of the margins they tried to confine us to. We're tired, yes. We're frustrated, absolutely. But we're also resilient in ways that don't require us to suffer. We're powerful in ways that allow us to rest. We're enough, exactly as we are, right now.

Keep going. Keep growing. Keep choosing yourself. Keep building community. Keep demanding better. Keep creating space for joy even in the midst of struggle. Keep protecting your peace like it's your most valuable asset—because it is.

Past me was right: there are bumps, detours, and moments of doubt. But there's also beauty, breakthrough, and moments of pure, unapologetic joy. There's laughter with your girls, there's music that moves your soul, there's food that tastes like home, there's love in unexpected places, there's success you worked your ass off for, and there's rest you finally allowed yourself to have.

We're not waiting for the world to give us permission to thrive. We're claiming it. We're living it. We're being it.

Still fierce. Still believing. Still unapologetically Black and woman and here.

With love, pride, and deep gratitude for the journey,

TT

October 2025

P.S. - That thing you're worried about right now? You handle it. That dream you think is too big? You're working toward it. That person who doesn't see your value? They're no longer in your life, and it's for the best. Trust yourself. You've got this.

The Unfinished Story

What We've Traveled Together

We started with letters to the future—hopeful, uncertain, determined missives from a young Black woman charting her course through rejection and growth, through relationship uncertainty and self-discovery, through societal weight and personal reclamation.

We moved through identity excavation—the deep, uncomfortable work of asking "Who am I?" and refusing to accept surface-level answers. We declared our names, our histories, our contradictions, our wholeness.

We explored personal branding—the gap between who we are and who others perceive us to be, and the intentional work of ensuring those align. We learned that reputation is what happens when authenticity meets consistency.

We witnessed reclamation—the transformation from silence to fire to self-worth. We saw how trauma tries to steal our voice, our body, our innocence, our story, and how we can reclaim every single piece through the sacred work of healing.

We celebrated multiplicity—meeting Alexis, Yvette, Loretta, and London. The personas that aren't masks but dimensions. The proof that containing multitudes is powerful, not problematic.

We mapped sanctuaries—Country Aire, Home on the Hill, and Bug. The physical and emotional spaces where freedom lives, where we can finally exhale, where home exists not as one place but as a thread connecting many.

What Hasn't Changed

If you're expecting this conclusion to tie everything up neatly with a bow, to announce that I've "arrived" at some final destination of self-actualization, I'm going to disappoint you.

Because here's the truth: **I'm still becoming.**

The viper of doubt still coils in my gut sometimes. The stranger in the mirror still appears on hard days. The performance of strength still feels easier than the vulnerability of asking for help. The personas still emerge when I need them. The sanctuaries still call me home when the world gets too heavy.

I haven't "overcome" my trauma—I've integrated it. I haven't "found myself" as if self is a static destination—I'm still discovering new layers, new dimensions, new possibilities. I haven't achieved some perfect state of authenticity—I'm practicing it daily, imperfectly, courageously.

And that's okay.

Actually, that's more than okay. That's the point.

What Has Changed

But here's what's different now, after all this excavation and examination and expression:

I know myself. Not perfectly, not completely, but deeply. I know my values. I know my triggers. I know my patterns. I know when I'm performing versus when I'm present. I know when to push through and when to rest. I know which battles are mine to fight and which aren't. I know my worth isn't contingent on anyone else's validation.

I trust myself. I trust my instincts. I trust my anger is information, not irrationality. I trust my voice matters even when it shakes. I trust I can handle whatever comes because I've already survived the unsurvivable. I trust my multiplicity serves me. I trust my healing journey is mine to navigate.

I claim myself. I claim my story without apology. I claim my anger without shame. I claim my sexuality without judgment. I claim my personas without pathology. I claim my space without permission. I claim my complexity without explanation. I claim my Blackness without dilution. I claim my womanhood without compromise.

I free myself. Not from struggle—that's still here. But from the need to perform struggle in ways that make others comfortable. From the obligation to be strong when I need to be soft. From the pressure to heal on someone else's timeline. From the expectation to forgive before I'm ready. From the demand to be one consistent thing. From the lie that my worth is earned rather than inherent.

This is the difference between where I started and where I am now. Not that life is easier or pain is absent, but that I'm equipped. Armed. Ready.

I know who I am. And I'm becoming more of her every day.

What I've Learned About Black Womanhood in 2025

This journey of becoming has taught me things about what it means to be a Black woman in this particular moment that I want to name explicitly:

Our strength is not our burden to carry alone. For too long, the "strong Black woman" archetype has been used to deny us care, support, vulnerability, rest. We're allowed to be strong AND need help. We're allowed to be resilient AND exhausted. We're allowed to survive AND still be wounded.

Our multiplicity is survival and strategy. Code-switching, persona-shifting, adapting to different spaces—these aren't signs of inauthenticity. They're evidence of our incredible adaptability. But we also deserve spaces where we don't have to adapt, where we can just be.

Our anger is righteous and required. They will tell you to calm down. To not be so angry. To rise above. To take the high road. But sometimes anger is the appropriate response to injustice. Sometimes rage is what fuels change. Our anger, when wielded intentionally, is transformative.

Our healing is revolutionary. In a world designed to break us, choosing to heal is an act of resistance. In a society that profits from our pain, choosing joy is rebellion. In systems that devalue our lives, choosing ourselves is revolutionary.

Our voices are powerful even when they're silenced. Every time we speak truth—even when it's not heard, even when it's dismissed, even when it's punished—we make it easier for the next Black woman to speak. Our testimony matters. Our stories matter. Our existence is resistance.

Our community is our lifeline. We cannot do this work alone. We need other Black Women who understand without explanation. We need chosen family who show up without being asked. We need spaces where we can remove the armor and still feel safe. We need each other.

What This Collection Asks of You

If you've made it this far, you've walked this journey with me. You've read my letters, declarations, testimonies, and truths. You've met my personas and visited my sanctuaries. You've witnessed my becoming.

Now I'm asking: **What about yours?**

This collection wasn't just meant to be consumed—it was meant to catalyze. To spark something in you. To make you uncomfortable enough to dig deeper. To inspire you to do your own excavation work.

So here's what I'm asking:

Write your letter to your future self. Where are you now? Where do you hope to be? What are you surviving? What are you becoming? Be honest. Be hopeful. Be real.

Create your identity manifesto. Fill in the "I AM" statements. Not who you wish you were, but who you actually are. All the contradictions, all the complexity, all the beautiful mess of you.

Audit your brand. Ask people what they'd say about you. See if it aligns with who you think you are. Identify the gaps. Do the work to close them.

Tell your survival story. However you need to tell it—in writing, in art, in conversation, in therapy. Reclaim what was taken. Transform your pain into power. Use your voice.

Name your personas. Give them birth certificates. Understand their purposes. Wield them intentionally rather than reactively.

Map your sanctuaries. Where do you feel free? Where can you breathe? Where is home—not just geographically, but emotionally? Return to those places when you need to remember yourself.

Do the work. The deep, uncomfortable, transformative work of becoming who you were always meant to be.

What Comes Next

This collection ends, but the becoming doesn't.

Tomorrow, I'll wake up and do this work again. I'll choose myself again. I'll show up authentically again. I'll use my voice again. I'll reclaim my space again. I'll become again.

Some days will be easier than others. Some days I'll feel powerful and clear and unstoppable. Some days I'll feel like that stranger in the chipped mirror, uncertain and anxious and barely holding it together.

Both versions are me. Both are valid. Both are part of becoming.

And the same is true for you.

You don't have to have it all figured out. You don't have to be perfectly healed. You don't have to be consistently authentic. You don't have to be always strong.

You just have to keep showing up. Keep doing the work. Keep choosing yourself. Keep becoming.

The Promise I'm Making

To my future self reading this years from now: I promise to keep becoming. To never stop growing, evolving, transforming. To honor all the versions of myself—past, present, and future. To protect the girl I was, to celebrate the woman I am, to make space for the woman I'm becoming.

To the Black Women reading this: I promise to keep speaking truth. To keep taking up space. To keep using my voice to amplify yours. To keep doing this work publicly so you know you're not alone. To keep fighting for our collective liberation.

To everyone who walks this journey of becoming: I promise to keep showing that it's possible. That survival is real. That transformation happens. That healing exists. That becoming is a lifelong journey worth taking.

The Final Truth

Here's what I know for absolute certain after writing this collection, after doing this work, after walking this journey:

You are not broken. You are breaking free.

You are not too much. You are more than enough.

You are not your trauma. You are your triumph over it.

You are not one thing. You contain multitudes.

You are not finished. You are becoming.

And that becoming—that messy, beautiful, painful, powerful process of discovering who you are and who you're meant to be—that's the whole point.

Not the destination. The journey.

Not the arrival. The becoming.

Not the finished product. The continuous creation.

The Invitation (One Last Time)

So here's my final invitation:

Become.

Become yourself—fully, unapologetically, courageously.

Become the person who speaks truth even when it shakes.

Become the person who claims space without permission.

Become the person who heals on their own timeline.

Become the person who contains multitudes without apology.

Become the person who knows their worth isn't earned but inherent.

Become the person who chooses themselves, consistently and without compromise.

Just become.

And when you do, write about it. Paint it. Sing it. Dance it. Share it. Because your becoming matters. Your story matters. Your voice matters.

Your becoming is part of our collective liberation.

So become, beautifully and boldly.

Become, messily and magnificently.

Become, powerfully and unapologetically.

Just become.

The Last Word

This collection started with a letter to my future self, uncertain about what was coming but determined to keep going.

It ends with a letter to all of us—past, present, and future selves—reminding us that the work of becoming never stops. And that's not a burden. That's the gift.

We get to keep growing. Keep evolving. Keep discovering new dimensions of ourselves. Keep becoming more fully who we were always meant to be.

I am Taria Patricia Fitch.

I am a letter writer and manifesto creator. I am a survivor and a thriver. I am Alexis, Yvette, Loretta, and London. I am Country Aire roots and Home on the Hill branches and Bug sanctuary. I am past, present, and future. I am healed and healing. I am powerful and vulnerable. I am one and I am many.

I am becoming.

And so are you.

To the stranger who became me:
Thank you for doing the work.

Thank you for surviving.
Thank you for becoming.

To the woman I'm becoming:
I trust you.
I believe in you.
I'm creating space for you.

To everyone on this journey:
You are not alone.
Your story matters.
Keep becoming.

The end is just another beginning.

Keep becoming.

Always.

With infinite love, unshakeable faith, and
unapologetic Black excellence,

Taria Patricia Fitch
Still Becoming
October 2025

A NOTE TO READERS

If this collection resonated with you, don't let it end here.

Do your own work. Answer the questions. Create your own manifestos. Map your own sanctuaries. Tell your own survival stories.

Share your becoming. Your voice matters. Your story could be exactly what someone else needs to hear to start their own journey.

Support Black Women. Not just in words, but in action. Believe us. Protect us. Amplify us. Give us space to be fully human—strong and vulnerable, angry and joyful, complex and whole.

Keep the conversation going. This is just the beginning. The work of liberation—individual and collective—continues.

Thank you for walking this journey with me.

Thank you for witnessing my becoming.

Now go become yourself.

Unapologetically. Courageously. Completely.

The world needs who you're becoming.

Thank You

To: _____

Thank you for holding space for my story.
Now I hold space for yours.

What are you becoming?

Remember: You are not broken. You are breaking
free.

With fierce belief in your journey, Taria Fitch.